A STRANGE SUBSTANCE!

Skunk-Guys foot kicked the clothes at his feet. He bent down and picked them up for a closer look. The fabric was full of burn holes and there were lots of goo stains. As he was examining the jacket, the stains jiggled strangely and skittered from the cloth onto his arm.

"Eeooow!" he bellowed, dropping the clothes and trying desperately to brush the goo from his sleeve.

The stuff wouldn't budge – it was anchored tight to his arm like barnacles on a ship's hull.

It was then that he felt something crawling on his leg. He looked down to see a mass of goo slithering from the fallen shirt onto his boot and up his leg.

He ran off down the street hopping on one leg while shaking the other leg frantically.

The Skunk-Guy series
NORMAN & THE STINKING SPACE GOO
THE SENSATIONAL SLIME SAGA

by Michael Wilhelm

Copyright © 2008 by Michael Wilhelm
Illustrated by Michael Wilhelm

ISBN: 978-0-615-25500-2

All rights reserved, which includes the right to reproduce this book or portions thereof in any form whatsoever except as provided by the U.S. Copyright Law.

All characters appearing in this are fictitious; any resemblance to actual persons living or dead is purely coincidental.

First Printing 2008

Printed in USA

CONTENTS

AUTHORS NOTE	vii
PROLOGUE	1
THE FAMILY TABLE	3
ON THE PROWL	11
ATTACHMENTS	19
ICKY STICKY GOO	27
A SPECIAL INGREDIENT	37
HAIR RAISING	47
IN SEARCH OF	55
STRANGERS	61
SLIP SLIDING AWAY	71
INTERRUPTION	83
FROM THE DEPTHS	93
THE BLACK & WHITE KNIGHT	101
FACING THE BEAST	111
EPILOGUE	117
SPECIAL NOTE	121
ABOUT THE AUTHOR	123

AUTHOR'S NOTE

Fort Wayne Indiana was a little different back in 1975. In an attempt to familiarize the modern reader with the customs of that era, I have scattered footnotes throughout this manuscript. I hope this will enhance your enjoyment of this truly gooey story.

PROLOGUE

A dark shadow arose behind the grate of a sewer drain along the street, and then oozed itself through. A distorted mass of goo, the size of a large cat, slithered its way across the road.

A car zipping by hit the dark fluid form, splattering it into a dozen small puddles. The residue of the splattered creature lay like rain on the street.

Slowly each little splotch began to flow across the surface of the road like melting candle wax, draining together into a single large puddle.

The surface of this new puddle began to pulsate up and down slowly, as though it were breathing. At last it pulled itself up as a single form again.

Another car roared past, but this time the ball of crud rolled out of the way. It was adapting to its environment. It was learning to survive. It flattened itself on the road as the wheels of another vehicle zoomed harmlessly over it.

Then this newborn slime thing pooled itself at the base of the curb and squirted up onto the sidewalk. With a slow wobbly motion it oozed its way along the deserted walkway.

It came upon an alley that reeked of stale beer and rancid meat. It stopped and savored the aroma. This putrid smell could mean only one thing: it had stumbled upon a snack. It oozed up the side of a brick wall and moved in.

In the clutter of the alley it was quite invisible. It blended right in among all the dumpsters and loose trash. It looked a lot like a smashed melon thrown against the wall.

Driven by the scent of decomposition coming from a large open dumpster, the goo critter slithered along the wall till it was just above the canister, and dropped itself inside.

It found within this large metal container a mass of spoiled food. The creature commenced to break down these materials into base proteins and sugars, which it absorbed into itself. It was feasting. It had found goo heaven.

Chapter One
THE FAMILY TABLE

The tangy scent of oregano, garlic and olives lingered heavily in the Flinches' kitchen. Janice Flinch's lasagna was a favorite with her family. Her husband Ed never had any trouble putting away several helpings. Their pretty blonde sixteen-year-old daughter Barbara would always put off any diet she was on in honor of the occasion. Now Norman, their gangly fourteen-year-old son, usually scarfed down as much as he could. Tonight however he was eating very little.

"Is something wrong, honey?" Janice asked him.

"No, Mom," he muttered through his milk glass.

"You're not eating very much."

Norman set his glass down. "Oh. See, I'm going out on patrol tonight and I don't want to be too stuffed. I may have to. . ." He sprang from his chair and landed on the floor in a menacing pose. "…You know, move quickly."

"Ah yes, Skunk-Guy," Ed acknowledged with a grin. "You don't want to be *weighed down*."

"Right!" Norman stated. "Only I prefer to be called the Stinking Stalker."

"You're going out again tonight?" Janice asked. "You've been out every night for the past three weeks."

"Well yeah, Mom. That's the idea. I'm patrolling the city looking for trouble. Well, not exactly looking for trouble," Norman corrected. "But. . . yeah I *am* looking for trouble, not to get into it, but so I can stop it. You know what I mean."

"Yes, I do," she said stiffly.

"In the past three weeks I've stopped vandals from toilet papering a house, and a group of taggers from writing graffiti all over some office building downtown."

"What about that Girl Scout troupe that attacked you?" Barbara chimed in.

"Yes, well…" Norman looked over at his sister with contempt. "That was an honest mistake. I came up out of the woods while they were sitting around a campfire. I was wearing my Stinking Stalker costume and it scared them so they jumped me. It was pretty ugly there for a few moments, but we all had a good laugh over it afterwards."

Barbara snickered.

"Don't forget I actually stopped a mugger from fleeing the scene of the crime," Norman pointed out.

"By throwing yourself in front of the thief," Janice said disapprovingly.

"I didn't do that part on purpose," Norman explained. "I tripped over that seeing eye dog. I tripped over the dog and the crook tripped over me. It was all very simple."

"So you say." Janice's tone was stern.

"And remember I'm the one who used my stink power to rescue Barbara from that jewel thief."[*]

"Which is the only reason I agreed to this whole absurd thing," Janice announced.

"I hope they throw the book at that creep," Barbara declared, brushing a strand of her long blonde hair over her shoulder. "I still wake up at night shaking because of what he did."

"You're still waking up at night?" Janice reached over and put her hand on her daughter's arm.

"It's not as bad as it was," Barbara assured her. "But still, being held at fork point is not something you easily get over."

"I'm just glad that your brother got there before something worse happened," Ed said. "The trial starts next month. Are you going to testify?" Ed asked her.

Barbara nodded. "Yeah."

"I am very proud of you both," their dad said. "It takes courage to stand up in the face of evil and demand justice."

"You've been reading my comic books again, haven't you, Pop?" Norman said with a knowing grin.

Ed felt his face blush. He looked over at his wife who glared at him.

---

[*] A tale aptly told in NORMAN & THE STINKING SPACE GOO

"Just a couple," he admitted, "I just skimmed through them. . . I didn't really read them exactly."

Janice shook her head and returned to buttering her bread. Ed took another bite of lasagna. The lull in the conversation gave Norman the opening he was looking for.

"Pop?" he asked cautiously. "Wendell and I were talking the other day and we think that The Stinking Stalker could use a base of operation."

"What about your bedroom?" Ed suggested. "If you ever get around to cleaning it up, you might find plenty of space for a command center."

Though his reasoning was sound, the idea did not sit well with his son.

"I'm going to need something quite a bit bigger," Norman explained. "Wendell figured out that if you dig a hole in the side yard, fifteen feet by thirteen feet and about twelve feet deep, then jack hammer through the side of the basement we can build a secret skunk-cave."

Ed looked at his son stupidly.

"Like that's going to happen," Barbara snapped.

"It could," Norman said without looking at her. "Dad's just thinking about it."

"Do you actually think he's going to demolish the side yard and blast through the foundation of the house?"

Norman turned to her and was about to protest when she interrupted him.

"You have a lot of good ideas, Norman, but you stretch them way out of reality until they become ridiculous."

Her words were so sincere that it caught him off-guard; she made him think for a moment. No, she couldn't be right; what would she know about this kind of stuff?

Their mother piped in with her suggestion. "If you cleaned up the storage room under the basement stairs you could set up a card table."

"Card table?!" Norman boomed. "Look, you guys, the Dragon Master has a secret lair in the tip of the Chrysler building in New York City. Captain Cosmo has an orbiting space station high above the earth."

"Lizard-Man doesn't have one."

Everyone at the table turned at the sound of Ed's voice. He had finally found the right words. "Neither does Electro Magma Man. And the Whispering Shadow has to change clothes in a phone booth."[*]

Norman relented with a sigh.

Ed looked over at his wife and winked. "See, there are advantages to skimming through comic books."

Norman took a last bite of his salad and pushed his chair away from the table.

"Where are you going?" his father asked.

"Getting ready to go out."

"Tonight is your night to load the dishwasher," Janice reminded him.

"But. . ."Norman protested.

---

[*] In 1975 there were no cell phones. In order to make a phone call away from home, you went to a small booth, provided by the phone company, which had a pay phone inside. You put 20 cents in the coin slot to make a 3 minute call.

"But nothing," Ed interrupted. "It's part of the agreement. You can go out afterwards."

"Okay," Norman mumbled as he picked up his dishes and headed toward the kitchen. Just as he was about to disappear around the doorway his dad called to him. He stopped and turned to face his father.

"With all that construction going on it would be very hard to keep that place a secret," Ed explained simply.

"Yeah," Norman groaned. "I guess we'd better come up with something else."

Ed gave his son a parental nod, and Norman went on into the kitchen.

༺ও༻

After kitchen duty Norman wasted no time getting up to his room to put on his Stinking Stalker suit.

Norman's bedroom was carpeted with all of his clothes folded in neat stacks. There was a path of bare floor that led from the door to the bed and the closet. This was done so that his enormous collection of comic books could be kept safe and secure in his dresser drawers. His closet was occupied by an old antique library card catalog. This was the filing system by which he cataloged and cross-referenced his comics. The only garment that he had hanging in his closet was his Stinking Stalker suit. It was neatly draped on a hanger that hooked on a peg behind the card catalog.

He slid on the black tights for his legs then worked his way into the tight-fitting body suit. It was white with holes for his legs to push through. The collar, shoulders and long sleeves of the garment were black. There was an insignia of a skunk head wrapped in its own tail emblazoned on the chest. He popped on his white boots and long white gloves, then slid on the pull over mask. It was a black mask with a white stripe that came to a point at the end of his nose. Two large netted white eyelets allowed him to see out while no one else could see in. He wrapped himself in the white pluming cape with its high pointy collar.

Inspecting himself in the mirror on his dresser, he struck a few heroic poses.

"None can face the awesome power of the Stinking Stalker," he proclaimed.

He spun around to watch his cape billow out and stumbled over his tennis shoes that he had carelessly tossed on the floor. He landed with a loud thud across a pile of shirts.

"You okay up there?" his father shouted up the stairs.

"I'm fine!" Norman answered back at the top of his voice.

Norman climbed stiffly to his feet. He limped over to the door and down the stairs. The Stinking Stalker was ready to prowl.

He stepped out into the kitchen where Barbara was talking on the phone.

". . .she said she thought the peach would be a good color but the peach satin was so expensive. It's really the hardest material to work with. . ."

She didn't even look up at her costumed brother when he came into the room.

He walked over to the back door and peered out cautiously. Satisfied that the coast was clear he reached over and turned the kitchen light off.

"Hey!" his sister protested. "I'm trying to talk here."

"You don't need the light to talk," he insisted.

"What's the big idea?"

"I don't want anyone to see me come out this door," he

whispered so that whoever she had on the other end of the phone would not hear him. "I don't want to give away my secret identity."

She rolled her eyes. "Oh, brother."

"Give me a few minutes to clear the back yard before you turn it back on."

"Just go," she ordered.

He stepped out into the night toward his quest.

Chapter Two
ON THE PROWL

A scraggly stray cat wandered into the back alley looking for some supper of his own. He was immediately startled by the pounding and sucking sounds coming from the large canister.

That particular dumpster had been the source of many a good meal. It appeared that another cat had already found whatever treasure was inside.

Challenged by this intrusion, the cat's hair bristled. He crouched down and sprang to the top of the dumpster, then dove into the open side.

Immediately the feline felt itself sinking into a burning oozy mass that seeped its way around it. The cat let out a yowl just as the lid slammed down over it. The inside of the dumpster began to glow with a gruesome green light.

❦

The Stinking Stalker was moving along quite briskly because he had a lot of territory to cover before his curfew. He wasn't being stopped by the police so much any more. They were getting used to seeing him prowling the streets.

The first night he had gone out, two officers had tailed him all the way to a break-in and apprehended a jewel thief. He was given kudos by the arresting officers who were both astonished and grateful for his efforts. It was then that his reputation as a crime fighter was established.

He was approaching a dark alley-way when he noticed fierce banging and pounding coming from the far end of the alley. He entered cautiously. The noise grew louder. He saw the dumpster and realized that some poor animal must have fallen in and couldn't get out.

"Poor little guy," he murmured.

He stepped over to the container and slowly lifted the lid.

A rocket of hissing fur shot out of the dumpster. It propelled itself right into his face, slamming him back into a pile of boxes, knocking both of them senseless.

After a moment the fallen hero looked up to see what had hit him. He couldn't tell what it was. It looked like a cat, sort of, except it was naked from the neck down — no fur except for the tip of its tail and its head. And he wouldn't swear to it, but the cat seemed to be smoldering. The alley was dark, but he thought he could see little wisps of smoke rising off the creature.

The animal staggered momentarily, then quickly regained its senses and ran off.

"That has got to be the ugliest cat I have ever seen."

He sat for awhile waiting for his heart to slow down. When he finally tried to stand up, his legs were wobbly. Then suddenly the dumpster lid slammed down. He jumped up and assumed an awkward fighting position with his fists drawn. After a minute of silence his adrenalin level dropped and his legs felt weak again.

He barely had enough time to take a deep breath when a woman's scream pierced the night air.

"Jumpin' crud!" he blurted out loud. "What in the world is going on around here?"

He scanned the area for the quickest escape route. Then it dawned on him why he was there in the first place.

"What am I doing?" he gasped. "I'm supposed to be the *hero*!"

With that he pumped up his courage, and ran out of the alley in the direction of the scream.

The lid of the dumpster jiggled and a green mass of gooey slime spewed out and ran down the front of the canister.

The creature now resembled an enormous swollen slug. It had tripled in size and had the mass of a full grown Saint Bernard. Its undulating, gelatinous form was encased in a purplish green membrane.

Suddenly it let off a sneezing, splat spewing an array of plastic, metal and other non-digestible materials onto the ground around it.

Though it was blind, the goopy monstrosity could sense the warm night air around it. Instinct dictated that it find shelter; it was far too vulnerable in the open.

It was tired, it needed to rest and digest.

Sluggishly it oozed itself out of the alley.

Rina Wells, the new late night disc jockey* at WIFF radio had walked several blocks in search of a pay phone. Her car had broken down on her way to the studio.

She stormed down the sidewalk in a huff. It was only her second night on the job and she was going to be late.

Finally she came upon one of those red turtle shell payphone units.** As she reached into her purse to get change, she felt herself jerked back by her own purse strap. The tug nearly wrenched her arm from her shoulder. She cried out in pain as much as in surprise.

She whipped around, and found herself standing face to face with a masked figure who had grabbed her purse strap. He was tall and bulky with a grungy ski mask pulled over his head and face.

She instantly clenched her hands onto the strap and pulled the purse away from him. He pulled back fiercely without uttering a word. As this tug of war continued she screamed at the top of her lungs hoping to attract the attention of anyone who might be passing by.

Finally from the corner of her eye she thought she saw a white blur racing toward them. She couldn't look directly at what was coming because she didn't dare pull her focus from her assailant.

Her screams must have drawn the attention of someone to help her.

Just then another pair of hands grabbed the purse strap and began pulling. A new masked figure had joined the game. This late comer was all decked out in a cartoonish, black and white outfit with a ghostly

---

* In 1975 radio announcers would use large black vinyl record albums. They would manually cue them up on a turntable, introduce the songs and entertain listeners between the music. These announcers were referred to as disc jockeys or DJs.

** These smaller units replaced the larger phone booths. They protected the phone from the elements but left the caller standing on the sidewalk.

white cape. She was outnumbered. Trembling with fear and anger, she mustered all the courage she could. If she was going to lose her purse, she wasn't going to lose it without a fight.

"Hey now, cut that out!" Rina couldn't tell which one of the two masked men had spoke.

"Stop it. This doesn't belong to you." The voice was insistent but not very persuasive.

Rina began kicking at the legs of her two challengers.

"Oww!" cried the voice again. "Hey! Ouch! Lady, I'm on *your* side."

It was at this point that one of the ends of the strap tore free of the purse. The purse now hung loose from the end of the strap that was held by the attacker with the grungy ski mask. He grabbed the dangling purse, pulling with all his strength against the strap that was held tight by Rina and the caped character. He anchored the purse under his arm like a football, turned his back to the others, and began a slow motion run, dragging his two opponents behind him. Their scuffling feet skittered along the sidewalk unable to find a foothold.

With a rip the purse pulled free of the strap. The released tension knocked Rina and her caped partner on their backs, while pushing the man in the ski mask forward so fast that he stumbled, tripped and plunged headlong onto the sidewalk. The purse flew out of his arms and into the air, landing with a PISH in the middle of the street.

The purse snatcher jumped to his feet, spotted the fallen handbag and darted out to get it. A car horn blast knocked him back on the curb just seconds from being hit. He was looking up and down the street gauging the traffic when he heard Rina's voice.

"You leave that alone!" she shouted, charging at him, her arms swinging wildly.

When she got close enough he shoved her back to the ground and ran off down the sidewalk and disappeared into a small recess between two office buildings.

This last landing knocked the wind out of Rina, and she lay paralyzed on the pavement. Her caped counterpart got to his feet and looked down the sidewalk after the escaped criminal.

"I think he's gone," he said. "We won't have to worry about him anymore."

He walked over to the woman on the ground.

"Are you okay?" He squatted down beside her. "Hi, I'm The Stinking Stalker. You may have heard of me."

She simply glared up at him.

"Anyway," he said, dismissing the awkward moment, "are you going to be okay?"

She rolled her eyes and shook her head in disbelief.

"Hey, at least he didn't get what he came after."

They both turned their attention to the purse in the street, just in time to see a car hit it. As the front tire rolled over it, there was a grinding crunch, followed by a soft POP when the rear tire went over.

Skunk-Guy got up, darted into the street and retrieved the mangled handbag. He brought it over to Rina, who was teetering to her feet. She quickly snatched the purse from him.

Without opening it, she shook it. A great deal of rattling came from within. She unzipped the top, peered inside for a moment, shook her head in disgust, then closed it back up. She looked over at the black and white superhero next to her, and began to beat him with the purse.

"You. . . you crazy goon!" she shouted.

Skunk-Guy held his arms up to buffer the blows.

"You moron . . . you . . . you . . . you busted my purse!"

Her last blow had enough force to knock him back a few steps.

"I was just trying to help you," he proclaimed.

"Dressing up in a costume scaring people to death is not at all helpful," she shot back.

"Let me at least escort you to where you need to go," he offered kindly.

"You stay away from me or, so help me, I'll mace you." Her threat was a bluff, she had already seen the nozzle on her mace can busted off and shattered in the belly of her purse.

"You keep as far away from me as you can, you gift-wrapped loony tune!"

The Stinking Stalker stood stunned watching the woman storm down the street. Her words did more to wound him than the blows with her purse.

Maybe, he thought, there *was* something wrong with him. No one else he knew paraded around in a goofy costume. Was he doing exactly what his sister said by going too far with it all? Had his interest in comic books really caused him to act irrationally?

He shook his head, dismissing the doubt. All this sounded too much like his mother and he knew *she* couldn't be right.

Just then he heard another cry – a man's voice this time. "Man!" Skunk-Guy exclaimed. "This town is going bonkers tonight." He ran off in the direction of the cry.

Chapter Three
ATTACHMENTS

A radio station is generally a pretty exciting place. There are lots of people around, music playing and everyone coming up with new ideas for promotions and contests. But late at night the place is dark and empty and maybe even a little spooky.

When Rina arrived she didn't even notice the spookiness of it. She was so upset; she just thundered across the empty foyer and took the elevator to the twelfth floor. She charged through the dark lobby of the radio station, making her way through the hallway of empty offices to the broadcast booth.

Through the picture window in the studio she saw Greg Stokes sitting at the console. The ON AIR light was not lit, so she walked on into the sound booth. Greg had his back to her and was wearing headphones.

When she tapped him on the shoulder he shot off the stool and spun around spastically. He dropped onto the floor and looked up at her with terror in his eyes, which faded when he recognized who she was.

"You're late," he finally said, untangling himself from the headphones cord.

Greg then noticed that the cute chick he had worked with last night looked awful. Her hair was wildly windblown, her coat was dripping wet, and she was in her stocking feet carrying her shoes and a flattened purse. She was covered from top to bottom with splotches of mud. She plopped the items down on the seat of the chair beside him. He noticed that the heel on one of her shoes was busted.

"I am so sorry," she said sincerely. "I am usually more professional than this. My car broke down and when I tried to call you, I was mugged. Then some creep who thought he was super-whosits tried to drag me off somewhere. I finally got away from him and then my heel got stuck in a sewer grate coming over here. This has not been a good night for me."

"Oh." Greg got up from the floor. "So where is your car now?

"Out on Clinton just south of Main," she stated. "It's a little red Dodge Dart with the hazard lights flashing."

"I'll call my auto club, they can tow it to a service station for you," he told her. "There will be a twenty-five dollar fee."

"That's fine." She dug through her purse and found her pocket book. She pulled it out carefully since it was dripping with red nail polish.

"Good heavens," he exclaimed.

She opened it slowly, letting it drip into the open purse. She pulled out a ten and a twenty-dollar bill, both smeared with red. "You accept cash?" she asked.

"Is it dry?"

"If you want I can dry them with the hand dryer in the restroom."

"You do that," he said. "I'll go ahead and put it on my card."

"Thanks, Greg," she said sincerely. "Give me a minute to dry off and freshen up. And I could use a cup of cocoa from the break room. You want some coffee?

"No. I've got a date and I'm already a half an hour late."

"What!" she gasped. "You're leaving me here, alone? You're supposed to be training me."

"I trained you last night."

"You're just leaving me here in this studio on the air by myself?"

"That's what you signed up for."

"I didn't realize that I would be *all* alone, what about a broadcast engineer who's going to be operating . . ."

He waved to her to be still. She saw the red light go on indicating that his microphone was now live. She intuitively stifled her protest in mid-sentence.

Greg spoke directly into the bright orange microphone.

"That was Booker T and the MG's with 'Green Onions'. The fact is, people, we can all rest easy now. Because our long lost lamb, Rina Wells, the new voice of Night Time Fort Wayne here at WIFF, has been found. She's a little the worse for wear, but she is still in one piece, and in fairly good working order. She's had a rough go of it this evening, folks, but she will be taking the controls at the top of the hour, have no fear."

Rina looked over at the digital clock on the panel it was 11: 52. She had eight minutes to pull herself together and be ready to read the local news report.

"But. . ." she peeped involuntarily, and then slapped her mouth closed. When she saw the light go out and Greg remove his headphones she resumed her protest.

"You're leaving me alone here in the station?"

"Yeah," Greg said matter-of-factly. "I wouldn't worry – you're probably the only one in the entire building."

At that, Rina felt her head begin to swim. When her eyes focused again she could see Greg staring strangely at her.

"Are you all right?" he asked.

"No," she blurted out. "I'm hyperventilating."

Just then she noticed the digital clock. She only had six minutes now.

"Ahhhh!" she screeched as she shot out of the booth and headed toward the ladies room.

※

The Stinking Stalker dashed down the street in the direction of the horrific cry. Someone was obviously in anguish. He had covered three blocks in little more than a minute when he stumbled across the tortured man.

The victim was lying on the ground tearing at his clothes, which were torn and smoldering. It looked as if someone had sprayed acid on the front of him. He was frantically ripping his jacket and shirt off while screaming, "I'm burning! I'm burning up!"

Skunk-Guy was stunned at the ferocity of the man's anguish. Then he realized that the man was wearing a grungy ski mask over his face. This was the mugger he had chased off.

Skunk-Guy jumped back as a powder blue police car[*] screeched to a stop, its siren blaring and lights flashing. Its doors flew open and two officers jumped out with their guns drawn.

"Hold it right there!" they shouted.

Skunk-Guy dumbfoundedly raised his hands.

"Oh," Officer Lewis said with a groan. "It's the incredible stinking boy again."

He lowered his gun and approached the man writhing on the ground. His partner kept his gun aimed at Skunk-Guy.

"What did you do to him?" the policeman asked as he examined the wounded victim.

"Nothin'," Skunk-Guy said. "I just got here."

"Argggg!" the fallen man cried as he rose up and pitched his garments away.

"Jerry, get over here and help me hold him down!" barked the officer.

"But what about. . . " his partner started to ask.

"Don't worry about him. He's supposed to be on our side."

Lewis looked over at the hero. "Don't move."

"Right," Skunk-Guy agreed solemnly.

The two policemen held the man down as he wailed and fought them.

"Hold still," the policeman ordered. "Oh my. . . Jerry, look at his chest – it's all burned. Get an EMS out here."

Jerry got up quickly and ran to the squad car. The man's goo-encrusted shirt and jacket fell at the feet of the Stinking Stalker. The

---

[*] The FWPD squad cars were all light blue back in 1975. No one really knows why.

hero didn't notice, however. His attention was riveted on the police activity.

"They're on their way," Jerry confirmed.

"Hold it down, pal," barked Lewis. "Help is coming."

"Bob?" Jerry asked.

"What?"

"Why is he wearing a mask?"

Officer Lewis looked up and for the first time noticed the grungy ski mask.

"Oh, this ought to be good," he remarked. "Would either one of you like to explain what is going on here?"

"He was trying to mug some lady and I chased him away," Skunk-Guy explained.

"Chased him away by spraying him with your. . . ." Lewis started to conclude.

"No!" Skunk-Guy interrupted. "I can't do anything like that. I mean that. . . that would be gross. All I can do is smell like things."

"Lovely," grunted Lewis. "Then how do you explain these burns all over him. Land sake's, his clothes are still smoldering."

"It was some kind of animal," the man gasped hoarsely. "I was running. . . and. . . I turned the corner. . ." The man winced in pain, gulped some air and continued. "I thought it was a huge dog. I ran right into it and then my body was on fire." He winced again. He lifted his head and pulled Officer Lewis down so he could speak directly in his ear. "It wasn't a dog, man." Then he passed out.

The cop pulled the ski mask off. He recognized him at once.

"Jimmy the Weasel. He broke parole last month." He turned to his partner. "We'll let the medics patch him up and we'll take him in."

His last few words were drowned out by the siren of the fire engine and the EMS truck. The two vehicles pulled up and the paramedics climbed out of their van and bent over the victim.

Skunk-Guy watched in silence as they took the man's vitals, treated his burns, loaded him on the gurney and hauled him away.

Officer Lewis stepped over to the Stinking Stalker. "Do you have anything more to say?"

Skunk-Guy thought a minute and said, "Good job, ya got him."

The officer looked the costumed hero up and down for a moment. "I don't know who you are in there, son. But let me give you a little advice. This is very dangerous work. You'd be better off leaving it to the big guys." He gave Skunk-Guy a severe gaze, then left.

Skunk-Guy watched the car drive off. He heaved a sigh of relief and started to leave. His foot kicked the clothes at his feet. He bent down and picked them up for a closer look. The fabric was full of burn holes and there were lots of goo stains. As he was examining the jacket, the stains jiggled strangely and skittered from the cloth onto his arm.

"Eeooow!" he bellowed, dropping the clothes and trying desperately to brush the goo from his sleeve.

The stuff wouldn't budge – it was anchored tight to his arm like barnacles on a ship's hull.

It was then that he felt something crawling on his leg. He looked down to see a mass of goo slithering from the fallen shirt onto his boot and up his leg.

He ran off down the street hopping on one leg while shaking the other leg frantically.

Chapter Four
ICKY STICKY GOO

The muck creature had shambled its way through downtown, and was working its way north on Lafayette. It was quite late and traffic on the road was very light. It had moved along about a quarter of a mile when it was caught in the headlights of an approaching car. The sound of squealing tires and a horn blast went unnoticed by this strange deaf glob.

A white sports car slammed full force into the gelatinous mound. The driver, a middle-aged man with graying hair and a goatee, was alone in the car. On impact he jerked forward, but his seatbelt locked before he hit the steering wheel. The momentum of the car propelled it into a spinning skid as it slid in the slime. When it finally stopped, the driver sat motionless. He was trembling inside and his chest hurt.

At last he took a slow measured breath, and peered for the first time at the windshield, which was splattered with purplish green running slime. He watched in amazement as the thick fluid drained itself off of the windshield, flowed down the front of the car along the hood, until all of it disappeared from view.

He unfastened his seatbelt and cautiously opened his car door. He stepped out and looked around at the front of the car to get a view of what it was he hit.

He was just in time to see the freshly reassembled blob ooze itself down the road and into a sewer drain.

"What the . . !" he gasped. "Did you see that? Did you see it?" He looked around, but no one else had. He was alone, the road was deserted.

∽⌒∽

The gunk had stopped moving on Skunk-Guy's leg but it wasn't coming off. He had tried rubbing it off and scraping it off but it was not budging.

"What is this stuff?" he groaned.

He needed help on this. This was definitely a situation for his partner, Wendell.

Wendell Higgins was the school nerd, a child prodigy with an I.Q. of 178. He had been instrumental in uncovering Norman's stink power. The two boys set up a buddy system of crime fighting: Norman did the leg work, wearing the costume and having most of the fun, while Wendell was the genius behind-the-scenes.

With this gunky sludge adhered to his arm and leg, Skunk-Guy was glad he had a genius to turn to. He took off his head mask and tucked it in his belt. Then he removed his cape and wrapped it around him covering most of his costume. He didn't want anyone, including Wendell's grandfather, to see Skunk-Guy coming over to his friend's house.

He moved as quickly as he could, staying out of sight as much as possible. It was a long clumsy journey. Twice he smacked himself in the face with overhanging branches, and once he soaked his foot when he stumbled into a small sink hole filled with water.

When he finally reached Wendell's driveway he leaned against the scrap iron mailbox.

"Made it," he sighed.

He readjusted his cape and walked up to the porch, climbed the steps and knocked.

Wendell's grandfather opened the door.

"Oh," the man said, recognizing Norman.

Norman smiled weakly as he held the cape tighter.

"Hi, Mr. Higgins. Is Wendell. . ? "

The older man nodded. "Go on up." He held the screen door open as Norman slid past him.

"That's a most unusual outfit you have on there, son," the man observed.

"Ah yes," Norman fudged. "It's Wendell's idea. Some kind of a science experiment. I don't understand the stuff he has me do half the time. But he sure is smart. Yes siree-bub, real smart." Norman made a hasty retreat up the stairs.

He charged through the bedroom door, slamming it closed behind him. Wendell, who had been tinkering with the circuitry of a citizen band radio*, fell off his chair.

"I'm in trouble," Norman announced.

"Hey, I thought you weren't ever going to come here wearing your outfit," Wendell commented as he got to his feet.

"I can't get it off," Norman stammered. "I was prowling around… you know, like I do… and I stopped a mugger. He ran off and the woman hit me… like, wham! Wham!.. with her purse. Then the mugger screamed and I went to see… and he was all burned… he was actually smoldering. He thought he ran into a dog…but it wasn't a dog. Then the goop jumped from his clothes and got on me and I can't get it off."

Wendell looked up at his friend through the thick lenses of his glasses. He was shorter than Norman and a year younger. He blinked twice, then finally asked, "What goop?"

Norman opened his cape, unveiling the rest of his costume. The crud on his arm and leg was pretty gross.

"This goop," Norman said.

Wendell stared at the substance. "What is it?"

"I don't know!"

"Does it hurt?"

"Not really."

Wendell stepped closer to examine it better. It looked a lot like melted purple candle wax that had splattered on his friend and hardened.

---

* Citizen Band or CB radios were all the rage back then. They are two way radios with 40 channels used heavily by truck drivers and motorists to communicate with each other.

He slowly reached up and touched it. Immediately he jerked his finger away with a sizzle.

"Owww!" Wendell cried. "Man, that burns!"

He held the wounded finger with his other hand. "It's acidic," he stated.

Norman's eyes grew wide. "Why isn't it burning me?"

"I don't know."

Wendell stepped over to his work bench and picked up a pair of needle-nose pliers. He went back to Norman and tried to grab a small piece of the substance. The pliers just oozed through it.

"Jumpin' crud!" Norman exclaimed.

Wendell thoughtfully rubbed his hand over his slicked-down red hair and stood holding the back of his neck for a moment.

"I want to try something," he finally said. "I'll be right back."

Wendell left the room and Norman attempted once again to try and brush the stuff off. When Wendell returned he was carrying a large box that contained some canisters.

"What's that?" Norman asked.

"Fire and ice," Wendell explained. "If one doesn't work, we'll use the other."

Wendell reached in the box and pulled out a blow torch and a lighter.

"What are you doing?" Norman asked with forced calm.

"In the tropics, explorers would expel leaches from themselves by using fire."

Norman cautiously eyed the blow torch. "You're not going to use that on me, are you?"

Wendell glanced at the torch. "Oh no," he assured him. "That would be a little over-kill. That just happened to be in the box. This is what I was after." He held up the lighter and flicked it on.

Wendell went over and squatted down beside Norman's leg. He flicked the lighter and held it up to the goo. The surface of the stuff began to fizzle and then the entire blotch skittered up Norman's leg settling onto his hip.

"Whooa!" both boys said in unison.

"Okay," Wendell said. "I've got an idea."

He stepped over to the box and pulled out an empty glass mason jar. He handed it to Norman.

"Here," he said. "Press this hard on your stomach with the open end toward the goo. I'll use this match to chase it into the jar."

Norman pressed the jar tight against his abdomen. Wendell flicked the lighter and drew it toward the goo. It started to sizzle and then it moved toward the jar. But instead of going in, the goo slithered along the side of the jar and hung on to Norman's chest.

Wendell directed Norman to move the jar up and beside the mass. Then he came at the stuff from the other side with the lighter.

The gunk slid its way up Norman's chest where it merged with the stuff on his shoulder.

"Wonderful," Norman moaned.

"Well, at least it's all together now," Wendell noted. "Now we move to plan B."

He searched through the box and pulled out a red fire extinguisher. He handed Norman a paper mask.

"Hold this over your nose and mouth," he directed. "And turn your head away."

Norman did as instructed and Wendell gave his shoulder a good blast with the extinguisher.

Norman cried out suddenly. "It's in my hair! It's in my hair!"

He was frantically tugging at the back of his head.

"Hey, look at this," Wendell said.

Norman stopped long enough to look over at his shoulder and there were a few small crystallized fragments stuck to his costume. Wendell reached up and pulled them off easily.

"I think we hit on something," Wendell concluded.

"Just get it out of my hair," Norman demanded.

"Easier said than done," Wendell explained. "I can't use the match because I will set your hair on fire. I can't push it out with anything because it will just ooze through it."

Norman groaned.

"Okay here's what we'll do," the whiz-kid declared. "I will spray it real good with the carbon dioxide. Then we'll cut it out."

"You're going to cut my hair?" Norman gasped.

"We've got no choice."

Norman sighed pathetically. "Don't cut too much," he pleaded.

"I'll do my best," his friend assured him. "Hold the mask over your face and hold your breath."

Norman took a deep gulp of air and held it in, then replaced the mask.

Wendell blasted the back of his head with the extinguisher for a good minute. After the fumes faded he examined the bulge in Norman's hair. He quickly nudged it. It didn't move. He hit it a little harder. It didn't move. He wacked it harder.

"Oww," Norman protested.

It didn't move.

"Terrific," Wendell declared. "We got it."

He quickly grabbed the wire cutters he had been using on the CB radio and began snipping his buddy's hair.

"Be careful," said Norman.

After much snipping and hair pulling, Wendell asked for the mason jar. Norman handed it to him. A few moments later Norman felt a weight drop off the back of his head.

"Got it," Wendell said with satisfaction.

"Let me see."

The boys stared with fascination at the purplish mass of gunk and hair stuffed in the jar.

"How much hair did you cut off?" Norman finally asked.

"Not much."

Norman reached behind his head and felt an enormous bald area leading from his neck to the middle of his head. He moaned.

"It was adhered right to the hair," Wendell told him. "I didn't have much choice."

"I'm going to look ridiculous." Norman dropped onto the lower bunk of Wendell's bed. "I can't comb over a patch that big. A hat won't cover it. And I certainly can't go around wearing a football helmet all the time."

"There *is* one other thing we might try."

"What?"

"Shave it all off," Wendell suggested.

"What, are you nuts?" Norman hollered.

"At least this way your whole head will match," Wendell concluded.

Norman looked up slowly then lowered his head in silent resignation.

"I'll get the electric dog clippers," Wendell said as he dashed out of the room.

Chapter Five
A SPECIAL INGREDIENT

Rina kept her headphones on constantly—that way she was able to drown out any strange noises she might otherwise hear in the vacant studio. She cranked the monitor up full blast whenever she had to leave the booth. She made every effort not to think about being alone in the empty building.

She got an idea that she hoped would make the long dark hours of the morning feel more secure. What she needed was someone to talk to.

After reading the local news at the top of the hour, she add a special announcement.

"I'm Rina Wells. The time is now 11:13 pm. Okay, we're going to do something different here tonight. I am new to your town and I would really like to get to know you.

"So I am opening the phone lines to take your calls. We can chitchat on the air and discuss any topic that may be on your mind."

She gave out the phone number and then played her opening song for the hour, "Crocodile Rock." She sat through that and three other songs and still not a single phone call. This was worse than she had thought. No one was out there listening.

"Don't be shy, folks," she announced between songs. "We'll talk about whatever you want to. It only takes one person to get the ball rolling." She looked over at the phone panel, nothing lit up yet. "I've got another good song lined up here. But if I don't see any phone lines light up I may be forced to pull out the elevator music."

She released the turntable and the Righteous Brothers' harmony filled her headset. Then she saw it, a little green light on the phone panel. She almost jumped out of her chair, she fought the impulse to stop the song right there, but she was a professional, she would wait. At last the song was over and she was back on the air.

"Okay we have our very first caller."

She pressed the button that played a tape recording of applause from an over sized tape cartridge. She flipped the switch on the phone panel for line number one, and tried her very best to make her guest feel at home.

"Welcome to WIFF Radio."

"Hello," came a man's voice into her headphones.

"Hello," she replied. "This is Rina Wells. Who is this?"

"Ah, Dave... oh no, wait," he stumbled with his words. "I was going to use a different... oh well, too late now."

"That's okay, Dave, we won't ask for your full name," Rina assured him. "So what would you like to talk about tonight?"

"You said we could talk about anything?" he asked meekly.

"Well, within reason and good taste," she clarified.

"You're probably going to think I'm crazy."

"Why?" she asked in all sincerity.

"Well. . ." He hesitated. "I saw something tonight."

"What did you see?"

He sighed loudly. "I was driving south on Lafayette Street earlier and I slammed into some kind of an animal."

"Oh," Rina squeaked. She hoped that this wasn't going to turn into a blood and guts story. "Did you hurt it?" she asked.

"No, but it tore up the front end of my car."

"Was it a deer?"

"No, that's just the thing. I don't know *what* it was."

"What did it look like?"

There was silence on the line.

"Dave, are you still there?"

"Yeah," he said softly, then repeated it a little louder. "Yeah, I'm here."

"What did it look like?" she asked again.

"Oatmeal."

"Huh?" she tapped her head phones to see if they were working properly.

"It looked like oatmeal," he verified.

"Excuse me," she said politely. "Are you saying 'oatmeal'?"

"Yeah, bluish-green oatmeal."

There was dead air for a moment while Rina regrouped her thoughts. Finally she asked, "How much oatmeal are we talking here, Dave?"

"Oh, I couldn't say." He gave a great sigh. "Probably several pounds."

"You're telling us that you drove your car into several pounds of blue-green oatmeal."

"That's about it, yeah," he confirmed.

"And you said it tore up your car?"

"Uh-huh."

"I see," she said thoughtfully. "So tell me, Dave, why did you call here tonight?"

"Well, I know you probably think I'm some kind of a kook. But that thing is still out there and I want to warn as many people as I can."

"The oatmeal is still out there?"

"Yeah," he insisted. "After I hit it, the thing shuffled off and slid down a sewer grate. It could pop up anywhere. I just thought people should be warned. It could be wounded and who knows what it's capable of."

Rina noticed that the phone lines were all lit up now.

"So you wanted to warn people about the wounded oatmeal under the streets?"

"Well," he coughed. "That's about it, yeah."

"Dave, I don't want to cast any aspersions on you, my friend, but I have to ask this. Were you drinking and driving?"

"No. I don't drink." Dave laughed nervously. "I was stone-cold sober. I had been working late and I was heading home and POW! It just appeared right in front of my car."

"Well, Dave, thank you for warning us. We'll keep a look out for the roaming oatmeal."

She switched off line one of the phones and flipped on line two.

"This is WIFF radio, and you're on the air with Rina Wells."

"Hi, Rina," a woman's voice said with sparkling excitement. "Hey, what a way to start! A man who drives his car into oatmeal." She laughed. "I was in tears. That was the funniest thing I have ever heard."

"Just the same, I am going to start carrying a spoon with me," Rina said suppressing, a grin herself.

"Look Rina, I wanted to talk about the time I was abducted."

"Abducted?" Rina blurted. "You were kidnapped?"

"By extraterrestrials."

Rina rolled her eyes and dropped her head. This was going to be a long night.

❧

A thin line of slime spewed out of a corrugated drainage pipe like a stream of saliva from a baby's mouth. It stretched itself down until it made contact with the bottom of the trench two feet below and pooled among the stones, dead leaves and rotted wood collected on the ground. This narrow finger of fluid grew thicker as it continued to drain. Occasional clots of scum would slide through, adding their mass to the puddle in the dirt.

After several minutes a greenish-gray mass of gunk appeared, filling the opening of the pipe. It remained still a moment then poured itself out and into the puddle below.

The weight of this enormous gelatinous mass sank it deep into the stones, twigs and debris around it. It was difficult to move through the clutter that filled the trench. It couldn't ooze or flow freely along as it had in the sewer or on the street. It had to push itself through knots of dead branches and undulate over large rocks. Sometimes, pieces of it would be pulled off and it had to stop and reflow back together. Progress was slow.

Eventually it discovered that it could hoist itself up over the biggest objects barring its path by utilizing the sticks and twigs. After a time it had gathered enough sticks that it was able to keep its entire form above the obstacles. Using these make-shift stilts enabled it to scuttle along much faster. As it advanced it resembled an enormous, deformed beetle.

As the morning sun began shining brighter through the trees above it, the mammoth creepy-crawly struggled up the side of the trench and onto the floor of the woods.

Although its other senses were evolving slowly, its sense of smell was rapidly growing more acute. It was overwhelmed by the odors that surrounded it; the musky moss, the pungent weeds and grass, as well as the stale sweetness of the dirt under it. Nothing of that nature interested it. This new-morphed insect was looking for something rank and foul, something that signified decomposition, which meant food.

Norman had called his dad, told him that he'd cut short his patrol, and asked if he could spend the night over at Wendell's. He did *not* mention why. His dad gave him the go-ahead, and the two boys poked and prodded at the strange slime most of the night.

At around 2:30 am Norman could hardly keep his eyes open and decided to crash on the lower bunk of the bed. Wendell was still going strong, for another hour he silently conducted a series of systematic tests. Finely he bellowed out in surprise, "Whoa!"

"Whaaat?" Norman mumbled, lifting his head groggily.

"You aren't going to believe this," Wendell told him. "I know what that stuff is and you're not going to believe it."

Norman's head felt cool, he reached up to rub his hair. He panicked the moment he felt only skin, but then he remembered.

"I'm not going to believe what?" he asked.

"I have been able to identify every element that this . . . gunk is made up of," Wendell explained. "It is not a single entity. It's really a colony of small life forms that are linked together and function as a single creature. A lot like a Portuguese Man-of-War."

"Imagine," he went on, "all these tiny bacteria and single cell organisms who are only capable of simple thought: eat, grow and multiply. Then thousands-maybe millions-of these creatures link their mental energy and are now capable of more complex thinking."

"How could that happen?" Norman asked.

"That's the kicker," Wendell expounded. "There is *one* element in here that is holding this whole thing together."

"What?" Norman asked, totally enthralled.

"I just happen to have an extra sample." Wendell stepped over to a small cardboard box on his work bench and pulled out a fragment of a shattered glass ball that was coated on the inside with a brown crust.

"That's the orb that I hit with the lawnmower," Norman said. "That's the thing that sprayed goop all over me."[*]

"It's the same stuff," Wendell declared. "The goop that gave you your skunk-like powers is the same goop that brought this. . .crud to life."

---

[*] Read all about it in NORMAN & THE STINKING SPACE GOO

"When Dad rinsed the stuff off of our house after my accident, it must have gone down the sewer and mixed with all the . . .eoww!" Norman gagged.

"We have a problem," Wendell told him. "See, there's a bigger version of that wandering around out there and we have to stop it before it hurts someone."

Norman involuntarily rubbed his hand over his head and asked simply, "How?"

"Well it's far too acidic for anyone to be able handle it." Wendell paused, then added, "Except you."

"Me!?" Norman protested.

"It likes you," Wendell stated. "Because you're made up of the same stuff. It probably thinks you're its mother."

Norman rubbed his head again. He had been doing that a lot since his haircut. "This isn't happening," he moaned.

"How about this for a plan," Wendell said with growing enthusiasm. "You memorize how that little puddle smells. Then you replicate it about a hundred times and draw the bigger creature to you."

"We have no idea how big this creature is, or how dangerous, " Norman stated. "And you want me to act as bait."

"You catch fire with fire," Wendell confirmed.

Norman walked over to the jar. "What do I do with it if I find it?"

Wendell pulled out a large fire extinguisher. "Blast it with this until it's frozen solid, then bring it back here."

"I'm not going to be able to carry a frozen muck monster around!

"I've got a wheelbarrow in the shed. Put it in there and bring it to the greenhouse out back."

Norman rubbed his head again. "This thing already got my hair. Who *knows* what else could happen."

Wendell studied his friend. Norman was still wearing his Skunk-Guy suit minus the cape and mask which he had tossed up on the upper bunk.

"Look at you," Wendell said. "Something weird and wonderful splatted all over you and changed you into someone special. Now *you* are the only one who knows about this terrible danger. You are the only one equipped to save the innocent people of this city."

Norman looked up and was about to protest when Wendell raised his finger.

"The fate of the entire world may come to rest upon a single noble heart."

It was a quote from the Solar Squadron comic book. Norman sighed, rubbed his head again and nodded solemnly.

Chapter Six
HAIR RAISING

When Norman got back home the next morning his mother was loading the dishwasher. In order to hide his Skunk-Guy suit he was wearing a pair of rubber fishing pants that belonged to Wendell's grandfather. He also had on a yellow raincoat with yellow rain hood that snapped under his chin.

He popped in the back door and tried to move swiftly through to his room.

"Hi, Mom," he mumbled.

Janice saw the yellow blur fly past her.

"Wait a minute," she ordered.

He stopped dead in the doorway not turning around. She was startled by his wardrobe.

"What are you wearing?" she asked.

"Oh, I didn't want anyone to see me in my suit. If they saw Skunk-Guy coming in here they would figure out who I am."

He didn't turn around to face her. She stood silent, then asked casually, "Did you and Wendell have a good time?"

"Yeah, we did," he said stiffly. "Great time. Thanks for letting me stay over."

"We appreciate you calling."

"I really need to get upstairs and get cleaned up."

"All right, go on."

He dashed up the stairs and collided with his dad who was coming down.

"Whoa son!"

"Sorry, Pop. It's hard to see in this hood."

"I can see that." Ed looked his son over. "Expecting a little rain, are we?"

Norman forced a chuckle. "Good one, Dad, that's funny."

Norman stepped around his father and darted up the last few steps, then into his room.

He closed the door behind him and took a deep breath. He unsnapped the buttons on the rain coat and dropped it on the floor. He climbed out of the rubber fishing pants. He stepped over to the mirror with the hood still in place. He unsnapped the flap under his chin and slowly peeled it off.

It gave him a queasy feeling each time he saw it. He rubbed his head again.

"It will grow back," he assured himself.

He put his robe on over his Skunk-Guy suit, grabbed a sweatshirt off of his shirt pile on the floor and a pair of jeans from the pants pile.

He grabbed some underwear and then draped the sweatshirt over his head, intending to sprint over to the bathroom and take a shower. He slowly opened his door and looked down the hall. The coast was clear. He darted out and ran straight into his sister who stepped out of her room. The two collided and the sweatshirt dropped. He bent down to get it and when he straightened up Barbara's eyes had practically popped out of their sockets. Her lips were moving but she wasn't making any sound.

Norman looked up at his forehead then back at his sister.

"Don't tell mom and dad," he told her. "I want to break it to them."

Suddenly she burst out laughing. She laughed so hard, tears streamed down her face.

"Please don't saying anything," he pleaded.

She nodded and waved him into the bathroom while wiping her eyes.

※

About an hour later, as Janice was unloading the dishwasher in the kitchen, she heard Norman bellow out from the dining room, "I'll be back later!"

"Wait a minute!" she answered back. "Come here."

"Uh...oh..." he stammered. "I can't right now, I'm really in a hurry." He stood around the corner of the door frame so she couldn't see him.

"You're not going anywhere unless you get in here," she demanded.

Norman rolled his eyes in surrender. He lowered his head and step around the door frame with his head down. He was wearing a pull-over sweatshirt with the hood pulled over his head. As he stepped into the room all she could see was the hood and very little of his face.

"What's wrong with you?" she asked.

Barbara, who was eating a salad at the counter, stifled a giggle.

"Nothin'," Norman mumbled as he rubbed his eye. "I got something in my eye."

"Here, let me see," Janice walked over to him, pulled his head up to look in his eye. The hood dropped down, revealing his bald head. Janice screamed before she could stop herself. She slapped her hand over her mouth. Barbara was jiggling with laughter.

"What. . . What did you do?" Janice gasped. "Your hair!"

"Yeah, I know." Norman blushed.

"I like your ears," Barbara teased.

Suddenly the back door flew open and Ed ran in.

"What's wrong?!" he cried frantically.

His gaze bounced back and forth to each one of them, then settled on their bald son. He studied the boy for a moment.

"Norman," he said quizzically, "wh. . .where is your hair?"

"It's over at Wendell's," Norman told him.

"Oh," Ed responded calmly. "And, ah, what is Wendell doing with it?"

"He threw most of it away," Norman admitted. "But we did use some of it to make a nest."

"A nest for what?" Barbara asked eagerly.

"Well, we don't know for sure."

"Is it a bird?" she pressed.

"No," Norman answered.

"Is it some kind of a squirmy reptile or rodent?" his mom asked.

"Not really. It's a kind of gooey blob creature."

"A blob creature," his father repeated

"Yeah. See it got stuck in my hair and Wendell had to freeze it out and then he cut it loose but he had to cut a big chuck of my hair with it. So then we just decided to shave my whole head. It doesn't look too bad, does it?"

Everyone just stared at him. Finally Barbara broke the silence.

"I'd start wearing a hat," she advised. "You could get a really bad sun burn up there." Then she took a big bite of crunchy lettuce.

"So how did the blob creature get into you hair, son?" his father asked.

"It jumped off some guy's jacket and climbed up my leg."

"That *would* explain it," Ed admitted.

"Hey listen, can I go now?" Norman asked. "Wendell and I need to figure out how we're going to trap the bigger slime creature that's running around loose out there."

"You want any lunch?" Janice asked automatically.

"I'm too excited to eat right now," Norman explained. "Besides, I'll get something over at Wendell's. Can I go?"

Ed looked over at his wife who made no response. He waved his son away. "Go on," he said.

"Great. Thanks." The back screen door slammed and Norman was gone.

Janice reached over and gave Ed a irritated slap on the shoulder. "We agreed that we weren't going to encourage him."

"I'm not, exactly," Ed protested.

"You said that you thought this was 'just a phase' he was going through, and that if we didn't make too big a deal about it, he would eventually give it up."

"Well, yeah, I did," Ed stammered.

"It's not working," she declared. "He's getting obsessed again."

"Now look," Ed defended. "I don't see any harm in enjoying this or any other phase as long as he's being responsible with the important stuff."

"And you have no problem with the effect all that comic book stuff is having on him?" she pressed.

"No, I don't," Ed stated boldly.

She pointed to the back door. "You think that's normal? Our son looks like a door knob."

"It's just a phase!" he exclaimed.

She shook her head in frustration, and went back to emptying the dishwasher.

"You have no idea how they're going to turn out when they get older," she murmured in a low voice. "You go out of your way to give them your love and attention and then something snaps." She slammed a cupboard drawer. "One day they're just as normal as anyone else and then POW!" She banged the pans as she put them away. "And no one else sees it, they all think there's something wrong with *you*."

Ed flinched as she slammed the dishwasher closed. She turned and spoke to him directly.

"He'd better not come home with a tattoo!"

Then she stormed out of the kitchen and up the stairs.

Ed looked over at Barbara for some support, but she had moved her salad munching to the dining room. He sighed deeply, shrugged and went back outside.

༺❀༻

Norman and Wendell had spent the day monitoring the citizen band radio Wendell had repaired, listening for anything that remotely hinted at an unusual occurrence.

There was one truck driver who had reported that he was positive he had plowed into a deer. But when he stopped and looked around, nothing was there except some slimy green oil dripping from his bumper.

Some farmer had reported that his dog returned home with its hair singed off and severe burns all over its body.

Campers in Fennerson's field were excitedly warning anyone who was listening, about a strange thing that had disrupted their camp early that morning. They said it looked like a blubbery insect the size of a cow.

Wendell had marked all three locations on a city map and drew a triangle connecting them. In the center of the triangle was an abandoned dairy, the perfect place for a wounded animal to go and hide.

"You're going to need to abandon your regular routine tonight," Wendell stated, "in order to hunt down this slimy thing."

"I *am* sort of responsible for it being alive in the first place," Norman admitted. "I guess I'm the one to get rid of it."

༺☙༻

When he mentioned at the supper table that he was going out to the old Fennerson's Dairy, his parents were hesitant.

"What do you want to go out there for?" his dad had asked.

"Well, we think we've found the big slime creature," he told them excitedly.

"At the old Fennerson's Dairy?" Ed questioned, while keeping a steady gaze on Janice.

"Yeah." Norman nodded. "So I'm going out there tonight and capture it."

"You and what army?" Barbara asked.

"I don't need an army; it thinks I'm its mother," Norman explained.

His mom dropped her fork with a clatter and got up.

"This is too upsetting," Janice said weakly. Then she gave Ed a glare full of fire. "*You* deal with it." Then she stormed out of the room.

Ed watched until she was out of sight and then dropped his head in frustration.

"It's okay, isn't it, Pop?" Norman asked.

Ed looked up and studied his son long and hard.

"Be very careful," he instructed.

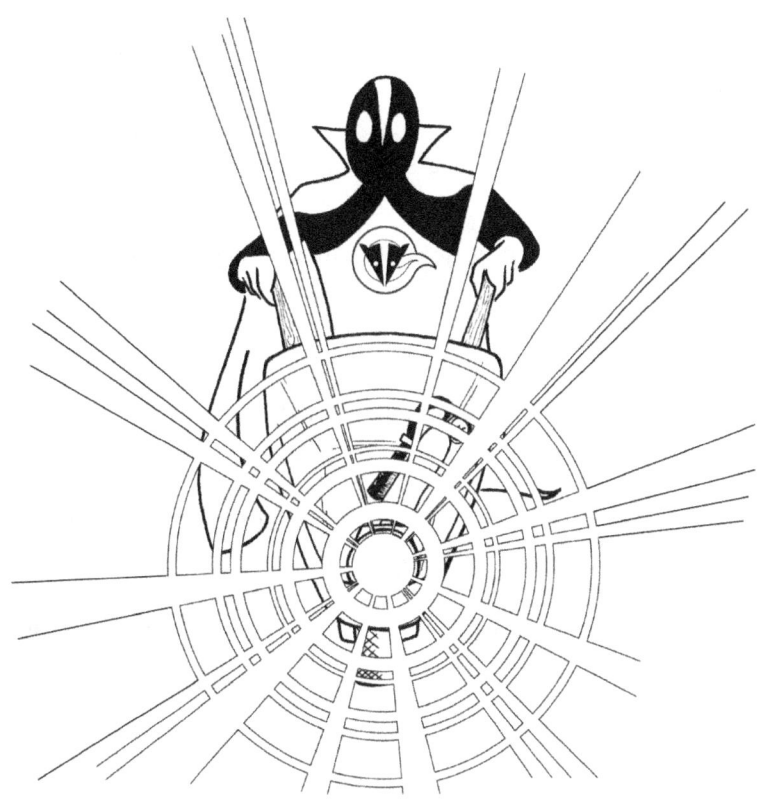

Chapter Seven
IN SEARCH OF

"You're listening to WIFF radio, something special on the air. This is Rina Wells, keeping you company throughout the night.

"I am opening the phone lines again, but before I do that I want to tell you what happened to me last night before I came on the air. I was mugged on my way to the studio. I fought the bum off. But I came face to face with another person who attempted to save me: a costumed character who looked like a refugee from a comic book. He was dressed all in black and white with a cape and mask, and he called himself stinky something.

"Now, I know I'm not crazy, but the station manager doesn't believe me. My program director doesn't believe me. In fact no one here at the station believes me.

"So I'm calling on you folks out there to prove me right. If any of you know of, have seen, or have met this stinky character, call in tonight and tell us all about it."

❧❦

Skunk-Guy went to retrieve the wheelbarrow he and Wendell had hidden earlier. The moon was full and gave just enough light to see by. However, the path looked a lot different at night and it took him a little while to find the exact bramble bush.

The sound of insects chirping and frogs croaking filled the darkness around him. He pulled the wheelbarrow out from behind the shrub and on to the path. He checked the items they had left in it, a fire extinguisher and a high-beam flashlight; both were there.

"All set," he said out loud.

He picked up the flashlight and shined it down the path into the woods. He noticed for the first time that there was a low misty fog drifting through the trees. He felt a cold shiver run down his spine.

"Whoa, there's nothing to be afraid of," he told himself. "The thing thinks I'm its mother." He thought about that a moment. "Why doesn't that make me feel better?"

He set the flashlight in the wheelbarrow so that its beam projected in front of it like a headlight. He gripped the two handles and headed off down the path deeper into the woods. He tried singing to himself but the tune was quivery and the words came out squeaky.

"Racing through the Universe,

Heedless of the danger. . ."

He stopped at the word danger and swallowed hard. He stood still, cleared his throat and tried to simply hum.

"Dum, De, Dum, De, Dum Dum..."

He decided not to sing at all.

He shined the flashlight beam all around him. He heard something skittering around in the underbrush.

Then a remarkable thing happened; he didn't jump. Instead, at that moment he felt a thrill race up his back. Excitement pumped him full of a strength he had never felt before.

"Okay, Mr. Muck Monster, you're about to meet your match."

He reached up and adjusted his mask. Since the loss of his hair the pull-over mask sagged quite a bit, and kept slipping.

He took the wheelbarrow in hand and journeyed deeper through the woods. He was headed toward an open cow pasture just north of town.

"Hi, Rina, this is Madge."

"Hi, Madge, how are you doing tonight?"

"Good, I'm doing good. Hey, I don't know anything about this Stinky guy you saw. He sounds an awful lot like my ex-boyfriend though."

"Did he wear a black and white costume?"

"Not really, he just hardly ever bathed. He was pretty stinky, if you know what I mean. He said it made him feel manly."

Rina slapped her forehead.

Skunk-Guy was on the edge of the Fennerson's property, the woods behind him and the overgrown cow pasture in front. He worked his way through the fog and high grass until he reached the dilapidated dairy. Leaving the wheelbarrow, he walked toward the building.

There were no doors, only two dark doorways, like missing teeth on a crooked smile. With flashlight in hand he stepped cautiously inside. The moonlight filtered through the doors and the holes in the busted roof. The fog had worked its way through the gaps in the wooden siding; it covered over any visible holes in the floor.

As the Stinking Stalker moved in, he was cautious where he put his foot down. The wooden floor groaned with each step.

His courage was starting to fade in the dark. He readjusted his mask and took a calming breath. He stood stock still.

"Okay mmister mmuck mmonsterrr!" he stuttered. "Mmommmmy's herrre."

Off to his right he heard something move, followed by a thundering metallic crash. This time he *did* jump and involuntarily flung the flashlight toward the noise. It landed several yards away on a pile of debris, where it slid down through a hole in the floor to the basement below.

Skunk-Guy was trembling. He tightened his jaw to keep his teeth from chattering. As his eyes adjusted to the darkness he could just make out the stalls where the cows used to stand. In one of them he saw the large shadow of something that was thrashing around wildly.

"This is Kevin."

"Welcome to the show, Kevin."

"Ya know, Rina, the whole thing last night could have been a fraternity prank."

"A fraternity prank."

"Yeah, they probably had some poor pledge dress up as a super goon and then they staged the mugging. The mugger was probably even in on it."

"I don't know. He wasn't the college type if you know what I mean."

"He was probably a theater major. I think I might know who it was."

"It had better not have been a prank," Rina scolded. "They ruined my purse and everything in it."

"Those pranks can get a little out of hand sometimes. Especially if they had been drinking."

"What's with the Stinky name, Kevin, how does that fit in?"

"It's probably Purdue University."

"I don't follow you."

"The initials PU."

Skunk-Guy could hear his heartbeat. He frantically looked around for the best avenue of escape. The door he had come through was a few yards behind him, but he couldn't see the floor clearly between here and there.

He shot for the opening anyway.

He emerged from the dairy so fast that he plowed into the wheelbarrow and somersaulted over it, knocking it over. The fire extinguisher rolled out and cracked him on the head.

"Oww!" he moaned.

He lay there only a moment. Then he grabbed the extinguisher, jumped to his feet and aimed it at the dairy door.

"This is Rina Wells, who is this?"

"I'm not allowed to give out that information."

"I see."

"But, I can give you my code name."

"What would that be?"

"Roswell."

"Uh, okay. So Roswell, what do you know about my close encounter with this stinky stranger?"

"He is really an alien and his true name is Stinkus. He escaped from a secret military base in New Mexico."

"Oh, I see. And you know this how?"

"I am a special agent for the US government."

"I don't mean to doubt you, but you sound awfully young to be a government agent. How old are you?"

"Uh. . . well that's top secret. Oh wait, my mom's com. . . I mean my supervisor is coming. Gotta go."

Click.

Chapter Eight
STRANGERS

Skunk-Guy stood poised for action for a very long time before he allowed himself to relax. It was obvious that whatever was in the old dairy building wasn't after him.

"Ya know," he muttered to himself. "that thing in there could be just as scared of me as I am of it." He felt another spasm of trembling go up his back. "Then again I doubt it."

"I've got to coax that thing out of there." He paused a moment to straighten his mask. "I'm not even sure it's the creature I'm looking for."

"If it *is* the creature, maybe I can draw it out by its own smell. Then I can blast it with the fire extinguisher."

He had memorized the smell of the small blob creature in Wendell's bedroom. After much practice he could perfectly copy the odor.

"And if it's some other kind of animal," Norman reasoned, "it will just stay in there and leave me alone."

He focused his attention and replicated the slimes own stench. He stood there reeking of sour sewer sludge for a long, long time.

He'd just decided that it probably wasn't the creature he was looking for, and that he had probably driven away whatever wild animal it *really* was. Then he spotted something move in the doorway.

He watched it, hardly blinking, mesmerized with a horrified fascination. The gunk-crusted slime creature stepped out of the dairy on rickety legs.

༺ஓ༻

"You're on WIFF radio, go ahead."

"Hi Rina, this is Bill."

"Hi Bill, what's up?"

"Look, I've got a theory about this Stinky person. I think he's probably someone who suffers from a mental disorder."

"Why do you say that, Bill?"

"Well, isn't it obvious? He's living out some costumed fantasy in order to overcome his own feelings of rejection. It's a typical text book case."

"Do you think he is dangerous?"

"I doubt it, he probably believes that he's really helping when in reality he's just making a spectacle of himself."

"You sound like you really know your stuff."

"I *am* a second year psychology student."

"I see."

"Hey, do you suppose I could get an interview with him for my term paper?"

"Well, so far, Bill, nobody seems to know who or where he is. If I were you I would just keep listening and take notes."

❧

Skunk-Guy didn't move; he hardly dared to breathe. The creature paused just outside the dairy door.

"Jumpin' crud!" he exclaimed softly.

It looked like some distorted beetle. It was roughly the size of a cow. The body was gloppy and wet-looking in the moonlight. Its legs were nothing more than tree branches and boards.

Then it began moving toward Skunk-Guy. It wasn't moving too fast, it was just coming closer, in the same way a horse might step over to another horse.

It reached the overturned wheelbarrow. It was close enough now for Skunk-Guy to see that its body was moving as if there were smaller things squirming around inside it.

He broke free of his amazement enough to realize that he was still holding the fire extinguisher. Then with renewed determination he blasted the creature with the cold white froth.

❧

"You're next on WIFF."

"Hi, I'm Phyllis."

"Glad you could join the fun."

"You know, Rina, you may have actually seen your guardian angel."

"If he was my guardian angel I think I got gypped."

"He protected you, didn't he?"

"In a matter of speaking. But, what angel in their right mind would call themselves 'stinky'?"

"Maybe it has some ethereal meaning. Did he say anything thing over you, like a prayer, or bring you a message?"

"Nope. He just chased the mugger away and then offered to escort me safely to work."

"Wow! What did you do?"

"I beat him with my purse and threatened to mace him if he didn't get lost."

"Rina, you may have committed a sin, striking an angel."

"I don't think he was an angel. But it probably *wasn't* a very nice thing to do. After all, he did try to help me."

"You may have provoked his wrath, Rina. He could put some kind of a curse on you. If I were you I would try and find him and apologize."

"That may be just what I need to do."

≈≈≈

Skunk-Guy sprayed the creature until the extinguisher was empty. He watched the caked frost on the figure slowly dissipate.

Its frozen form shimmered in the moonlight. It started to lean to one side, then it fell over.

Skunk-Guy leaped in the air in triumph.

"Yess!" he proclaimed to the sky.

He stood over the fallen figure. Satisfied that it was sufficiently subdued, he grabbed the wheel barrow. He set it back up and then stepped over to the creature.

"Okay, big guy, time to take a little ride," he said as he bent down.

He put his arms around the frozen gunk and attempted to lift it. It was too heavy. His arms just slid across its icy surface.

"Come on," he groaned as he tried again.

Still he couldn't move it. After two more attempts failed, he began to notice that the surface wasn't quite as solid as it was. This thing was thawing out. He had to move fast.

Quickly he moved the wheelbarrow around to the other side of the blob. He set it on its side and tried to roll it into the wheel barrow.

He wasn't getting anywhere so he stood up and pushed it with his foot. His foot began to slowly sink into the softening goo.

He jumped back and the critter quivered and jiggled and eventually got back up on its misshapen legs.

"I don't suppose you could just jump in there for me?" he asked it.

"Hi Rina, this is Carol."

"Hi Carol, welcome to WIFF."

"I like your new show."

"Glad to hear it."

"I was wondering, do you think that this person who helped you might be some kind of a weird boy-scout?"

"He sure didn't look like a boy-scout."

"Well maybe not actually a boy-scout, but a member of some other group of young men who earn merit badges by doing good deeds."

"Like Stink Scouts?"

"Maybe. He might be just one of an entire league of heros."

"No. Believe me, Carol, this guy was one of a kind."

With the wheel barrow between him and the gunk creature, Skunk-Guy felt a little safer. The thing was standing still.

Skunk-Guy adjusted his mask again. The blob beast took no notice of his movement. It simply started backing away toward the dairy.

Skunk-Guy watched greatly relieved and then he realized that he had stopped making himself smell like the slime sample in Wendell's room. He resumed the odor and to his astonishment the creature jerked to a halt and began moving toward him.

He stopped the smell again. This time it was to determine whether that thing was really able to smell him.

The muck monster stopped dead. It didn't move for quite awhile then finally headed toward the building. Skunk-Guy revived his smelly condition and the critter changed its direction immediately.

"I got it," Skunk-Guy announced to no one in particular.

He grasped the handles of the wheel barrow, turned it around and headed back through the pasture. The deformed animal followed after him.

Skunk-Guy traveled slowly enough so that it could keep up with him. It followed him through the tall grass and into the woods like a well-trained ugly pet.

෯

"Welcome to WIFF radio."

"Hi Rina, this is Randy."

"Hey there, Randy. So do you have any thoughts about who that masked man was?"

"Well not really, I just want to know: what did he smell like?"

"Oh, ah, well. . ." Rina fudged for the words while she considered the question. "Come to think of it, Randy, he didn't really smell like anything. Of course you have to understand that I was pretty upset, I wasn't in the mood to go smelling anybody."

"With a name like Stinky, I would have thought that he would have. . . you know, stunk."

"Well, I am glad he didn't."

"You could have heard it wrong. Maybe his name was Kinky or Dinky or even Blinky."

"I may have been upset at the time, but when someone dressed up like a six-foot skunk comes up and tells me his name is Stinky, I believe it. That's what he looked like, come to think of it. He looked like some kind of a super skunk."

"Super Skunk?" Randy repeated as though he were tasting something awful.

"Sounds crazy, huh?"

"Kinda, yeah."

"Maybe it is. No one seems to have heard of this guy. He appears out of nowhere and then disappears again," Rina went on. "If it wasn't for my trashed purse, I *would* think I was nuts. He has got to be out there somewhere. And I promise all of you listening; I am going to find him."

The trek through the woods was a lot harder without the flashlight. The full moon had risen higher in the sky, dimming its brightness.

He checked back frequently to make certain that his misshapen companion was still following him. It was right on his heels.

Eventually they cleared the woods and were now on the edge of the Higgins back yard.

It resembled more of an open field than a yard. No grass had been planted. Natural flora grew wild. A footpath was all that was maintained.

Skunk-Guy stumbled onto the footpath which wound around to the greenhouse.

This small glass building had a crumbly brick foundation. Its glass-paneled walls and roof were fogged with grime and age. Ivy covered a good portion of the south end of the structure. It housed several long tables, where dozens of plants were being nursed by Wendell's grandfather.

Parking the wheelbarrow around the side of the greenhouse, the Stinking Stalker stepped over to the glass paneled door. He held his hands up, gesturing to the gloppy thing to stay put.

"Stay!" he commanded.

He tapped on the glass. After a few moments, one of the doors opened and Wendell stepped out.

"Did you find it?" Wendell asked.

"He followed me home. Can I keep him?" the hero joked.

Wendell's eyes came very close to popping out of his head, an action that was exaggerated even more by his thick glasses.

"My gosh! What in the world? Incredible!" Wendell stammered. He just stared at it for a long moment. "It's bigger than I thought."

"Yeah, he wouldn't fit in the wheelbarrow," Skunk-Guy explained. "So I got him to follow me. I'm not sure that he can actually see, but he can smell pretty good."

"I have never seen anything like it," Wendell murmured.

"Let's get him inside," Skunk-Guy directed.

The boys entered the greenhouse followed by the misshapen mound of walking goo.

Wendell closed the door behind it.

"Did you bring the other one?" Skunk-Guy asked.

"It's on that table over there."

Skunk-Guy spotted the aquarium. He went over and lifted the lid. Gently he reached in and picked up the small lump of sludge. It nestled in his hand.

As he walked back toward the big creature the blob in his hand began jiggling wildly. Suddenly Skunk-Guy screamed and dropped the glop on the floor. The tiny slime ball slithered quickly across the floor and up the legs of the bigger monster, oozing itself into it, disappearing for good.

"Look at this!" Skunk-Guy cried, holding out his hand.

The fabric of his glove had fresh burn holes and his own skin was blistering.

"What could that mean?" Skunk-Guy puzzled.

"It means that it doesn't think you're his mother anymore," Wendell stated.

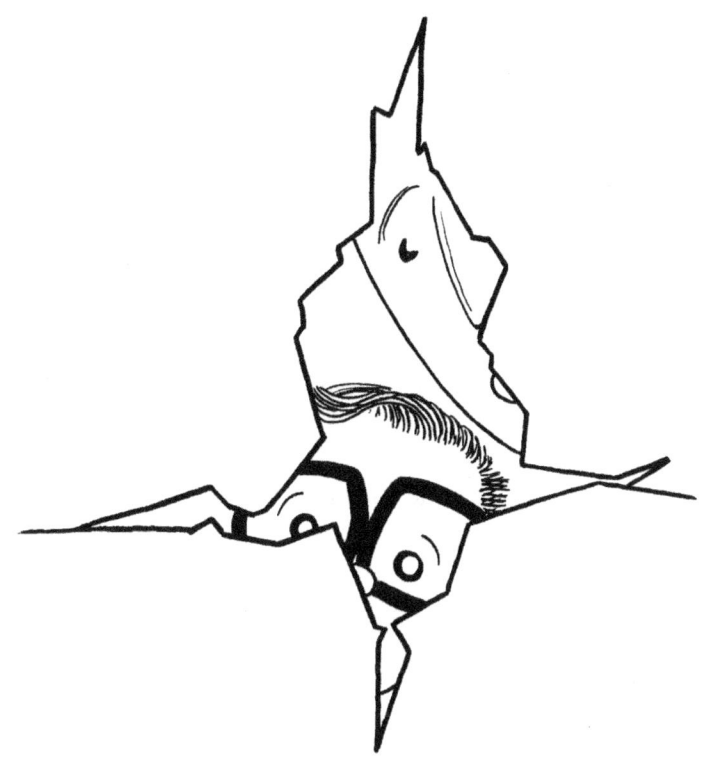

Chapter Nine
SLIP SLIDING AWAY

The next morning was bright and cheery. Sunlight filled the Flinches' kitchen while Ed sat at the table and scanned the newspaper.

As Janice entered the kitchen, Ed watched her over the top of his paper. She filled a cup with some coffee then sat down at the table.

"Did Norman get in on time last night?" she asked.

"He was a little late, but he called from Wendell's and told me."

"Good." She took a sip of her coffee.

"Could you put the paper down?" she asked. "I want to talk to you."

"Talk away. I do some of my best listening while I'm reading," he teased.

"I'm serious, Ed. I want to talk to you before the kids come down."

He dropped the paper and gave her his full attention.

"I'm all ears."

"You don't seem to see the seriousness of the situation," she began. "Norman is obsessing with his comic books, and I'm not sure where it could lead."

"It's just a phase," Ed said exasperated.

"You sound like a broken record," she snapped. "Our son wears a weird costume and runs around the city every night. This is not normal behavior."

Ed gave his wife a gentle grin. "Honey, we used to tie a towel around his neck and he would ride his bike around with it flapping behind him. He loved it."

"He was six then," Janice pointed out. "He's fourteen now. If this is a phase it's an awfully long one."

"You're hard to follow sometimes, honey," Ed spoke firmly. "You worry about him sitting around all summer reading comic books and not getting out and doing stuff. Then when he does get involved and finds something that motivates him to be more responsible, that freaks you out."

"These are his early teen years," Janice explained. "These are the years that will define his character and self-perception. How is this going to affect him when he reaches adulthood?"

"You got your new woman's magazine this month, didn't you?" Ed asked.

"That's beside the point," she stated. "I am concerned about the influences affecting him. You remember back in the late 50's? Comic books were banned by the government because they were a bad influence on kids."

"They've debunked all that since then," Ed defended. "There *is* some nasty stuff out there, but for the most part the stuff he reads is Truth, Justice and the American way."

"But it's blurring his ability to know what's real and what isn't."

"Norman is not stupid," Ed retorted. "He has a special talent and he's having fun with it."

"But..." she started to say.

"Come on," he said. "Let your hair down. Play along for a while. Who knows, you might just have fun, too."

She looked at him severely and rolled her eyes.

Just then Norman thundered down the stairs.

"Mom," he whined from the dining-room. "Tell Barbara to hurry up. I want to call Wendell."

"You're just going to have to wait," Janice shouted back. "She needs to make plans for the day, too."

Norman burst into the kitchen. "Yeah, but she takes so long. Oh, hey, Pop."

Ed looked up.

"We got that slime creature," Norman said. "You should see it. Man, it's about this big, and this wide, and it's all slippery and slimy-like. And it walks around on sticks and boards for legs. It looks like this huge bug. It's really cool."

Janice looked over at Ed, panic stricken. He gave her an encouraging smile.

"That's nice, dear," she forced herself to say.

"You'll never guess where it came from," Norman asked.

Ed and Janice shared a bewildered glance and then Ed shrugged.

"From you, Pop," Norman announced. "All that goo you sprayed off of the house when the lawnmower blew up. It flowed down the sewer and brought all the sludge and goo to life somehow."

Janice gave Ed a frantic glance. He held his hand up in a gesture of peace.

"So when you think about it, you're really responsible for the creation of a new life form. Hey, maybe they'll name it after you, call it *Ed Fungus* or something."

"Well, it's a good thing you caught it," Janice said stiffly.

"What are you going to do with it, son?" Ed asked.

"We're not sure. We probably ought to destroy it. It's kinda dangerous," Norman explained.

"Dangerous?" Janice squeaked.

"It's pretty acidic. You can't touch it or it will burn you," Norman told them. "Wendell wants to keep it alive and use it for next year's science fair. I'm anxious to see what it looks like in the daylight," he admitted.

Ed looked over at Janice as he asked, "Well, how about if your mom and I go with you? Wouldn't you like to see a real life slime creature, honey?"

Janice looked stricken. She nodded reluctantly.

Norman was dumbfounded. "Really."

His gaze bounced between his folks several times, then he said, "Cool. I'll tell Wendell."

He darted out of the kitchen and up the stairs.

"Barb, will you hurry up!" he shouted.

The car pulled into the Higgins driveway, rolling past the scrap iron mailbox. Ed parked it up by the garage door.

The Flinches climbed out and walked up to the porch.

"Look at this yard," Janice said as she surveyed the jigger bushes, weeds and nettles growing wild on the property.

"Wendell doesn't have to worry about yard work," Ed noted.

"You might be surprised, dad," Norman answered.

They stepped up to the front door and Norman knocked. Almost immediately the door popped open. Wendell's grandfather opened the screen door and invited them in.

"Hi folks," he said. "I'm Willard Higgins."

"I'm Ed Flinch, this is my wife Janice, and you know this guy." Ed put his hand on Norman's shoulder.

"Norman has become quite a fixture over here," Mr. Higgins told them, "which is fine with us. You know, up to this time, Wendell pretty much stayed in his room a lot. I didn't think he had many friends. But they seem to be having a lot of fun together. They have apparently started some new secret club."

"You mean they haven't told you. . ." Ed was interrupted as Norman let loose with a loud obnoxious cough.

Ed looked over at his son, and then he realized that he had almost given away Norman's secret identity.

"We were hoping you could tell us what they're up to," Ed said, covering his mistake.

Just then Wendell stepped into the living-room. "Hey," he said to Norman.

"Hey," Norman nodded to his friend. "These are my parents."

"Oh. Hi."

"Hi," they replied.

"It's nice to finally meet you," Ed told him.

"We've heard so much about you," Janice added.

"The boys have some kind of scientific project out in the greenhouse," Mr. Higgins announced.

He led them out the front door. Wendell grabbed a fire extinguisher from the front closet as he left.

The group made their way down the path, through wild grass and past a twisted oak tree hung with several bird feeders.

"We've got wild raspberries over there," Wendell's grandfather pointed out. "And over there is some mint. We have over eight acres. Most of it is woods. My father planted all the rest of this when he built the place. He wanted to make it in to a natural garden. It may not look it, but tending to this place is more work than a conventional yard."

They walked for some time; the house was quite far away now. The path followed along the edge of the woods, then made a sharp turn to the left. The greenhouse was straight ahead. It looked creepy even in the daylight.

"It's in there, Dad," Norman said excitedly.

The boys ran ahead and Wendell unlocked the doors.

"Okay, now," Norman announced. "This thing is pretty gross and dangerous so be careful around it."

"Maybe you should let your father go in first," Janice suggested.

Ed nudged her arm. "I think the boys can handle it. Go on, son."

The adults followed the kids inside. Everyone stood still and scanned the interior of the greenhouse. There were several tables of plants lining the walls. There were lots of sticks and branches strewn across the floor. But there was no sign of any strange creature.

"Where did it go?" Norman asked Wendell.

"I don't know. I locked it in here last night."

"This is not good," Norman said.

"How could it have gotten out?" Wendell wondered out loud. "I'll look around."

As Wendell started investigating the shop, Norman turned to the grown ups.

"It was a really weird slimy blobby thing. It was about as big as a cow and it used those sticks and boards as legs"

"I'm just as glad that I didn't see it," Janice confessed, holding her hand up to her mouth.

"Find anything, Wendell?" his grandfather asked.

Wendell had crawled under one of the tables and was hidden from view.

"Over here, Grandpa," he answered.

They all walked over to the table as Wendell pulled it away from the wall.

Half way up the wall was brick and mortar. The top of the wall had glass panels that fitted in to a wooden framework that rose and arched over their heads.

"Look at this." Wendell directed everyone's attention to the brick foundation.

There was a large hole in the wall where several bricks had dislodged and the mortar was eroded away.

"It must have slipped through there," Wendell said.

"How could something as big as cow get through that?" Janice asked doubtfully.

"It was like pudding, it could change its shape and slip on through," Norman explained.

"Oh, I see," Janice said giving her husband a skeptical look.

"Sorry to have dragged you folks out here on a wild goose chase," Willard Higgins said.

"That's okay," Janice said with relief in her voice. "We've been wanting to meet Norman's new friend and this seemed like as good a time as any."

"This is not a good thing, Grandpa," Wendell explained. "That thing is made up of all sorts of corrosives and acids. It can very easily break down the molecular structure of any living matter."

"What did he just say?" Ed asked.

"It can burn things with its touch," Norman said. "Especially skin."

"Ahhh," Ed acknowledged with an exaggerated nod. "I thought it was something like that."

Since there was no apparent danger, Janice felt safe enough to get into the playfulness of the game. "Gee, I wonder where a cow-sized glob of walking jello would go."

"It's attracted to strong odors," Wendell explained.

"The Three Rivers Festival starts tomorrow," Mr. Higgins said. "There'll be all sorts of strong odors there."

Wendell began a list of things that could attract the creature. "Popcorn, stale cotton candy, beer. . . and tons of dumpsters overflowing. Just the sort of thing to draw the attention of a hungry glop thing."

"My goodness, this looks like a job for. . ." Janice started to say but was cut short as Ed elbowed her in the ribs.

"Don't overdo it, honey," Ed told her softly.

"That doesn't give us much time to find it," Wendell concluded.

The night before, under the cover of darkness, the creature had oozed its way out of the hole in the greenhouse wall and slithered deep into the woods. It was slow going at first without its legs. It did eventually gather enough new sticks for it to walk again.

It frantically scuttled around looking for some nourishment till well past dawn. It wasn't as easy to find food in the woods. There just wasn't as much available in the forest as in the trash bins of the city.

Eventually the heat of the sun forced the...thing to find a cool hiding place in the hollow of an old gnarly oak tree. Even though it could not find any food, it was able to rest there unprovoked throughout the day.

It wasn't until long after the sun set that the hidden goo creature was lured from its hideaway.

From somewhere nearby a dog yelped, then came the drifting musty stench of putrid skunk. The poor dog's whimpering echoed through the woods.

The hidden blob jerked and jiggled with excitement. This new odor brought hope that at last food was not far away.

Belteshazzar, a 71-pound Labrador/German Shepherd mix, was rolling on the ground in a vain attempt to rub the skunk oil from his coat. His nose and eyes were throbbing.

The mammoth creepy-crawly scuttled right up to the dog like a spider after a fly caught in its web. It stepped over the rolling animal and began to spew itself down onto the dog.

At the first touch of the slime to his coat, the dog yelped and jumped to its feet, knocking the creature's wooden legs to the ground.

The dog shook the slime from him and turned on his fallen attacker. He ran in circles around the glob pile, bouncing and jumping around it. He barked angrily, interrupted by an occasional sneeze brought on by skunk musk.

The goo started pulsating, and slowly began to grow. It needed to appear larger than its attacker. It reconfigured the sticks on the ground to form an internal skeleton for itself. It was now standing about five feet tall.

The dog leaped back with his tail between his legs; his barking stopped. The two of them stood stock-still. The dog tried to stare his enemy down, but the creature didn't have any eyes to focus on.

The gloppy beast then moved forward, lifting one foot, taking a step. The dog began a deep guttural growl. The creature lifted the other foot slowly and took another step. The dog barked and bounced backward.

The slime creature followed after the dog, who was still barking incessantly.

✥

Isaac Mueller had been trying to drift off to sleep for some time now, but his dog's barking outside was taunting him.

It wasn't unusual for Belteshazzar to bark at night—in fact it made Isaac and his wife Grace feel protected. But this barking sounded different. It was frantic and it had been going on for quite a while.

"I'll go see what he's riled up about," he told Grace as he climbed out of bed and shuffled to the window. He lifted the pane a little higher and peered through the screen.

He could just see his dog bounding out of the woods at a fearsome trot. The dog spun around snarling at the woods.

It was then that a black figure stepped out of the woods and stood menacingly on the boundary of his yard.

"Sakes alive," he scoffed. "Someone's down there pestering him. Probably one of the Fike boys, been out drinkin' again."

He stepped into his slippers and grabbed his shotgun.

"I'll be back," he told her. "Keep the bed warm."

When he stepped out onto the front porch he called his dog. "Balty, get over here. Come on, boy!"

As the dog approached he got a whiff of the skunk musk. "Sakes alive! Wheeew! Go on, get outta here. You go on now."

His eyes were watering. "Get in the barn, boy. Go on in the barn."

Tail between his legs, the dog obediently walked into the barn.

Isaac then drew his attention to the figure standing outside the woods.

"Is that you, Roy? . . . Butch? Now you boys leave poor Balty alone. You go on home now."

The figure began to move toward the barn.

"I said, you go on home now." Isaac held up the shotgun.

Whoever it was ignored him and continued to head to the barn. He hated the idea of shooting one of his neighbors. He lowered his gun and ran over to the stranger. He stopped dead in his tracks a few feet away when he realized that it wasn't a person.

"What in tar-nation?" he gasped.

The thing, or whatever it was, kept moving to the barn.

Isaac fired two blasts of buckshot into the thing.

The creature jerked spastically, then remained motionless.

Isaac slowly moved to the side of the barn. He fumbled for the high-pressure hose he used for irrigation. He aimed the nozzle, opened the feed valve, and let it fly.

The water pressure drove the creature back. Isaac backed the walking gunk all the way into the woods until it was out of sight.

He stood there for quite a while waiting for the thing to emerge from the trees. It never did.

"What will that dern dog drag home next," he thought.

～⚭～

After being chased off of Mueller's farm, the walking mound of muck stumbled its way through the woods. It staggered through the trees and brush. It was almost invisible in the dark.

It was desperate for food. It needed quite a bit more to sustain its new larger upright form, but it found nothing to consume. It was getting weaker with each step. Its outer form was growing crusty and scaly.

It banged recklessly into trees and stumbled over plants and wild grass. It had more and more difficulty remaining upright. It sagged pathetically, losing strength to move on.

It began a slow-motion tumble forward. It collapsed over a tree stump and slid down a cliff, then dropped below the surface of the St. Joseph River with a soft splooosh. The reflection of the moon rippled across the surface of the water.

Just as the water was starting to settle, the slime creature bobbed to the surface. It floated like a putrid island drifting down stream. As it traveled it soaked up a great amount of river water that caused it to grow heavier and heavier. Eventually it started sinking lower and lower in the water until it finally dropped below the surface and settled on the bottom of the river, a highly infectious pile of slime.

Chapter Ten
INTERRUPTION

    The Three Rivers Festival was a city-wide, nine day celebration commemorating the three rivers that flowed through Fort Wayne: the Saint Joseph, the Maumee, and the Saint Mary's.

    The festivities began with an opening day parade in the morning that stretched through the downtown area. Crowds lined the streets for miles in eager anticipation of the procession.

    This was the first year that Skunk-Guy would make an appearance—not as a parade participant but as a protector of the people.

He patrolled the outskirts of the parade route carrying a fire extinguisher. He diligently searched for any sign that the *thing* would be attending.

Skunk-Guy had stayed out extra late the night before, trying to track down the oozy fugitive, with no luck. It was still out there somewhere.

He hoped that the creature would show itself soon. There were so many events planned throughout the next nine days, he would easily exhaust himself trying to attend each one in order to keep the crowds safe.

Many of the people who spotted him assumed that he was part of the program.

Several little kids began following him. In very short order he had quite a crowd of children tagging after him. Moving through the crowd was getting more difficult.

"Hey mister, who are you suppose to be?" one of the kids asked.

"I'm the Stinking Stalker," he answered.

"Man, that is so lame," the kid shouted back.

"Can you fly?" asked a little girl.

"No, I don't fly," Skunk-Guy explained kindly. "I stalk. . . I stalk around. See, I'm the Stinking Stalker, and I'm stalking around looking for trouble makers."

"What are you going to do with *that*?" another child asked about the extinguisher.

"Oh, nothing," he said.

The crowd of youngsters was pressing in on him. He felt like he was going to drown.

"So what's your super power?" That kid's voice sounded familiar.

"I can stink," he said.

"That's a stupid power," the kid shouted.

"Would you like to see a demonstration?" he asked the kids.

He was greeted with a chorus of yes's and cheers.

"All right then." He stood still and let them gather around him. "Here goes."

Suddenly the stench of rotted hamburger mixed with the sting of putrid fish filled the air.

The kids all grabbed their noses and ran away screaming.

"You're listening to the Three Rivers Festival live, here on WIFF. This is Jake Seavers coming from our mobile broadcast booth here at Freiman Square in downtown Fort Wayne, the heart of the Three Rivers Festival.

"We have a veritable sea of people surrounding our booth here. And it just so happens that WIFF's newest late night star, Rina Wells, is here on the street with microphone in hand to capture all the excitement. Rina, are you out there?"

Rina had been listening for her cue through a portable transistor radio[*] she had borrowed from someone in the crowd.

"I'm here, Jake. This is my first time at the Three Rivers Festival and I must say I am quite overwhelmed."

"Did you get to see the parade this morning, Rina?"

"No, Jake, about the time the parade started up I was going to bed. I have the night shift, you know."

---

[*]MP3s and IPOD's had not been invented yet.

"Well, I saw it and it was just wonderful. The best one yet as a matter of fact. So where are you right now?"

She moved the radio from her ear and raised the microphone to her mouth.

"I am on the corner of Clinton and Main watching the crowds of people drifting through the many event booths set up along here. Maybe I can get someone to say a few words."

She looked around at the people immediately in front of her and held out the microphone as an invitation. Finally two girls walked over.

"Hi," they said into the mike.

"Hi, I'm Rina Wells with WIFF radio. Are you having fun?"

"Oh yeah," one of the girls remarked. "We come here every year, this is my fourth time."

"What is your favorite event?" Rina asked.

"The parade was very good this year," the other girl said.

"But hands down my favorite is the raft race,"[*] the first girl stated.

"Now, I have heard. . ." Rina stopped a moment. She thought she heard someone scream. She quickly passed it off and went on with her thought. "I heard they were going to have a *bed* race."

The girls giggled.

"Oh yeah," the second girl said. "That should be pretty . . . "

She was interrupted by another scream coming from the middle of the intersection.

"What in the world. .?" Rina spoke, forgetting that she was broadcasting on the air.

---

[*] The raft race was a part of the Three River Festival until 1996 when it was discontinued.

"Rina, Rina this is Jake in the booth. What's going on out there?"

Rina raised her voice in order to be heard over the wild screaming. The entire crowd was fleeing in terror.

"Oh, ah, I don't know for sure, Jake. But people are running frantically away from the intersection. There may have been some kind of an accident. I'm going to try to get a look."

What she saw made her gasp so loudly that everyone listening on the radio thought she had passed out.

She watched as an incredible amount of what looked like bluish green sludge was erupting out of two man holes centered in the intersection.

"The killer oatmeal," Rina gasped across the air waves.

"The killer what?" Jake asked.

"It really is real," she said to herself.

She snapped out of her shock suddenly and jerked the microphone up, hitting herself in the mouth.

"Ow! oh, sorry," she said. "You're not going to believe this, folks, but there is a huge mass of bluish slime oozing out of the sewer below us."

"Bluish slime?" Jake repeated. "You're kidding, right?"

"It's not just oozing out but it seems to be chasing after people."

She watched as the gunk spread itself like a huge oil spill. The edge of it had reached the curb where she was standing and was slithering up onto the sidewalk.

At that moment a panicked pedestrian plowed into her, knocking her to the ground. The transistor radio went in one direction and the microphone went flying in the other.

She couldn't get up because too many people were running wildly, practically trampling over her. Then she caught sight of the creeping glop heading straight for her.

She could hear sirens approaching but they would never reach her in time.

Suddenly she was hit in the face with a wild blast of cold. She instinctively turned her head away. For a brief second her head was spinning and she couldn't breath. It felt as though her throat closed up. Then in the next instant her head was clear and she was gasping in a lung full of air.

She turned back to see what it was that had hit her.

"I don't believe it!" she gasped.

Between her and the deadly goo stood a black and white figure, with a white cape that was flapping in the wind. He was blasting the gunk with a fire extinguisher.

It was him. It was her guardian angel. He had done it again. He appeared out of nowhere and was fighting for her life.

The fire department had set up four pumper-trucks and was rinsing the goo off the street with fire hoses.

The goo was easily diluted into a gross soupy mess.

Rina stood up and over the sound of the panicked crowd and the thundering water shouted to Skunk-Guy, "Thank you!"

The Stinking Stalker looked back over his shoulder.

"You okay?" he shouted back.

She nodded gratefully.

"This stuff freezes the goo," he started to say. "Whoooaaaa!"

A powerful blast of water from a fireman's hose blew him down the street. One minute he was there, the next he was gone.

"Sorry!" a fireman shouted.

Rina stood bewildered in the cascade of water spraying around her. So much had just happened.

The firemen quickly worked their way up to where she was. They were spraying the slime up Clinton street.

"Get out of here, lady!" one of them ordered.

"What are you doing?" she shouted, trying to be heard over the sound of the spraying water.

"We're hosing this stuff up the street and off the bridge into the St Mary's river," he explained. "We'll run it through the filtration plant. That should take care of it."

"Are you sure that's going to work?" she asked.

"It's the best idea we could come up with on the spur of the moment," he barked.

"Do you even know what that stuff is?" she hollered.

"Sewage. Why, what do you think it is?" he shouted back.

"I don't know," she admitted. "But that other guy, the one you blew away, seemed to know what it was."

The fireman grinned, "That cornball has a lot more problems than backed up sewage if you know what I mean. You'd be better off just going home and drying off."

"What if he's right?" she insisted.

"I'll take my chances," the fireman said. "Now beat it."

"This is Jake Seavers coming to you live at the tragedy here in Freiman Square. People are running past the broadcast booth in a blind panic. The devastation all around us is indescribable. We lost contact with Rina Wells in the midst of all the commotion.

"I am alone here. I shall stay here till the end. I will continue to broadcast as long as I can speak and as long as the power holds out."

"Wait..." He spotted Rina running toward the booth. "We have reestablished contact with Rina Wells. Perhaps she can give us an eye witness account of the catastrophe."

Rina charged into the broadcast booth. Jake stuck the microphone directly in front of her.

"Rina, tell the WIFF audience everything you know about what's happening out there."

Rina looked at the microphone, then she looked up at Jake. "The sewer backed up," she stated simply. "The fire department is hosing it out into the river."

"The sewer backed up?" Jake asked unbelieving. "That's all?"

"It will be cleaned up in a jiffy," she said.

Rina picked up a clipboard with a chart typed on it. She scratched her name off and headed back out the door.

"Where are you going?" Jake screeched.

"I'm going to try and find my guardian angel," she announced as the door banged closed behind her.

❦

After tumbling a block and a half, Skunk-Guy ended up wrapped around a street lamp post. He opened his eyes and discovered that he was blind. The blow on his head must have affected his vision. Panicked, he cried out and grabbed at his eyes.

Then he realized his mask had slipped again and that he was looking into the black fabric. He slid it back around and lined up the eyelets of the mask with his eyes. He breathed a deep sigh of relief, feeling very foolish.

The first thing he saw was the fire department spraying the goop off the bridge and into the river.

"Huh," he thought, "I suppose that could work."

"Could it be that simple?" he wondered out loud.

He was banged up, wet, tired and bald. This hero business was doing him in. He had been up all night trying to out-think a mushy monster, and in just a few minutes the fire department had the situation taken care of. He felt pretty small.

After all, under that costume he was just a kid. It would take a lot more than this fancy costume to make a hero out of him.

Sure he had found the slimy thing *but* it also got away from him.

"Am I really cut out for all this, or am I just play-acting, like Mom said?"

He needed to rethink it all. He decided to just go home.

Chapter Eleven
FROM THE DEPTHS

After being sprayed off of the bridge and into the St Mary's river, the slime that had erupted from the sewers was now swimming or slithering through the water like an eel.

Although the fire department had assumed that the goo would be carried downstream and into the city filtration system, the stuff was actually moving upstream under its own power.

All of it was driven up the river by a powerful instinctive urge, similar to that of a salmon swimming upstream to spawn. It swam for miles like an enormous black cloud in the water.

The journey was long and hard. It was getting difficult to hold itself together in the water. The gunk swam lower and deeper as it moved.

At last it knew that the journey was over, and dropped to the river bottom wrapping itself around a mound of slime that was sticking up from the muddy floor.

After all the muck had settled, the mound was more than three times its original size. As the old and the new slime merged, life came back to the fading goo.

If you had found yourself swimming in the water around this enormous muck pile you would have noticed a distinct rise of temperature. In fact, the water was getting pretty hot.

Then you would have noticed that there was an eerie green glow filling the murky water. But since you weren't swimming down there, you missed all that.

The glow faded and the mound quivered wildly. Gradually it stopped. It appeared motionless for a long time. However under the surface it was quite busy rebuilding itself.

Finally it rose up on two enormous slimy legs. Its full height was now almost nine feet tall. It concocted for itself two misshapen arms. These uneven bulky appendages had web-like flippers at their ends serving as crude hands. From all the litter polluting the water a couple of glass bottles had wedged themselves into the dark gunk. These allowed the beast to see light for the very first time.

Through these new glass eyes it spotted jittery light flickering above it —the sun shining through the surface of the river. The creature was fascinated. It sprang upward propelling itself through the water. The light grew brighter and brighter. It poked its misshapen head out of the water.

WACK! Without warning something clubbed it from behind. It turned sluggishly in the water, swiping at whatever it was that had hit it.

~~

Janice tossed the Skunk-Guy suit in the washing machine. She turned some knobs and pushed a button and water sprayed onto the garment. Suddenly she was grabbed from behind in a playful hug as Ed spoke softly in her ear.

"You wanna go goo-hunting again today?" he teased.

She pulled away coldly and gave him *the look*.

"This whole thing is ridiculous," she said. "Our son has an overactive imagination. So instead of teaching him to grow up and get a grip on reality, you're encouraging him to go off and fight goo monsters. The worse part is you got me doing it."

"But wasn't it fun, just a little?" he coaxed.

"Excuse me if I don't get excited about playing goo monster," she snorted.

"That was something, wasn't it?" Ed mused. "I almost believed it all."

"You let him stay out far later than normal," she scolded

"But he did come in when he promised," Ed pointed out.

"Then he stayed up all night talking to Wendell on the phone," she added.

Just then Barbara flung open the basement door.

"Excuse me!" she interrupted frantically.

They both looked up the stairs at her.

"You guys might want to see this," she told them. "Something is going on that has Norman's finger-prints all over it."

They darted up the stairs and followed her through the house into the living room.

The television was on. Local news reporter Dan Turnley was on the screen. He was standing outside in front of a hectic scene of fire trucks, police cars and construction equipment. There was an excited crowd gathered around him.

"...the police have chased the crowd away from it. They have a call in for the curator of the children's zoo to come out and look at this thing, this creature, in the hopes that they can identify what exactly it is.

"We're going to play back the film of the creature coming out of the river."

The picture changed to a grainy image of the raft race in progress. Suddenly the lead raft crumbled as though it had smashed into a rock. Then a very large misshapen creature was seen swimming to the left bank of the river. As the beast climbed out of the water people began running and shouting. Some ran away, others ran toward the slimy gunky thing that now walked like a man.

Ed and Janice slowly turned their gaze toward each other as the reality of it all came bursting in on them.

"Where is he?" Ed asked.

"Upstairs sleeping," Janice said hesitantly.

"I'll get him," Ed told her.

He climbed the stairs to his son's bedroom.

Norman half staggered, half stumbled groggily down the stairs. He was trying to rub the sleep from his eys.

His mother and his sister were sitting on the edge of the couch staring intently at the TV. Ed stood next to the recliner eager to watch his son's reaction. Norman rubbed his eyes and tried to follow what was happening on the tube.

Dan Turnley was interviewing the people around him.

"... I don't know, man," commented one teenage boy. "I just saw this big walking blob, man. It was huge, like ya know what I'm saying? And I thought, man, this is one big piece of garbage and it's like walking around, ya know. The thing blew my mind."

Norman's eyes grew wide, very wide.

Dan Turnley turned to a couple of young girls wearing Three Rivers Festival t-shirts.

"What did you two see?" he asked.

"Well, first it smashed the raft," one girl explained. "And I thought, like wow, that was a pretty lame raft."

The other girl piped in, "Then this slimy creature poked his head out of the water and I lost it. I screamed so loud I scared her."

"Then I screamed," the first girl admitted. "And it was like we were all screaming and it was getting pretty intense."

"Then the thing climbed out of the water and it was huge and slimy and I screamed again."

"Then *I* screamed again. And then, like, everyone was running around screaming. It really freaked us out."

Dan instructed the station to show the photo of the creature.

Norman was wide awake now. At the sight of the huge creature his mouth dropped open and "Jumpin' crud!" leaped right off his lips.

"This is the unexpected guest who disrupted the raft race," Dan's voiceover explained. "It is roughly nine feet tall and made up entirely of... well, we're not quite sure.

"We do know that three people have been hospitalized with severe chemical burns after touching the... thing."

The picture changed to a live shot of Dan. A young dark-haired woman was standing next to him.

97

"I know her," Norman blurted out. "I helped her twice, once the other night and then again this morning at the parade."

Dan turned to the woman. "Now you said that you were looking for someone?"

"Yes, I am," Rina Wells stated directly.

"Did someone get lost in the crowd?" Dan probed.

"I hope not," she said. "We can't afford to lose anyone with that much courage."

"Who was it?"

"My guardian angel," she confessed. "I don't know his name. I think it's stinky something."

Anger flashed across Dan's face. "Is this some kind of a joke, young lady? Because if it is, this is a very bad time to. . ."

Rina interrupted him. "It's no joke. I think that it's some sort of a nickname. Anyway this hero went out of his way to protect me a couple of times. He was even able to keep that slime at the parade from crawling all over me. He seems to have some knowledge of what that thing *is* out there. I'm surprised that he's not here right now offering his help to the police and fire department."

"Yesssssssss!" cried Norman, leaping up punching the air with his fist.

"Noooooooo!" cried his Mother standing defiantly.

Everyone in the room stared at Janice.

Norman was stunned. "What's the problem?"

"What are you, crazy?" she stammered. "That thing is. . . is . . . huge. You saw it. It's nine feet tall."

"And it burns people," Barbara pointed out.

"I can handle it," Norman said. "I did it before."

"That how you lost your hair?" Barbara quipped.

"Face it, I'm the only one who knows what it is," Norman argued.

"It's nine feet tall," Janice repeated.

"They need my help, you heard it."

"What could you possibly do that the police and fire department couldn't?" his mother demanded.

"I got it to follow me home," he stated. "Of course it was a lot smaller then and it did think I was its mother. But the fact is, it knows me."

His mother sat dumbfounded then blurted out again, "It's nine feet tall."

"He might be able to help them control it." They all turned to Ed as he spoke. "It would be like sending a bee keeper in to move an unwanted hive. He wouldn't be going in to show off. He would only be going to work along with the police and fire department as an advisor. Wouldn't you, son?"

"Huh?!" Norman choked out. "Oh yeah, right, that's right. . . That's it, an advisor. Please, Mom?"

Janice let out a deep sigh, gave Ed an icy glare and then reluctantly nodded.

"Yessssss!" Norman cried, repeating the fist-pumping leap. This time however he cracked his shin on the edge of the coffee table. "Oww!" he moaned, grabbing his wounded leg and hopping around on the other.

"Watch it, big brother," Barbara giggled. "The town needs a hero who isn't beat up before he comes to the rescue."

"Where's my suit?" Norman winced.

"In the washer. It's probably soaking wet," Janice told him. "At least let me dry it."

"I can't wait, Mom. The city can't wait."

"It wouldn't take more than half an hour," Janice said, moving toward the kitchen.

Norman followed her all the way down the stairs. As his mom pulled the costume out of the washer he grabbed part of it from her.

He looked her resolutely in the eye. "The fate of the entire world has come to rest upon a single noble heart."

His mother rolled her eyes and tossed the rest of the suit at him with a wet splat.

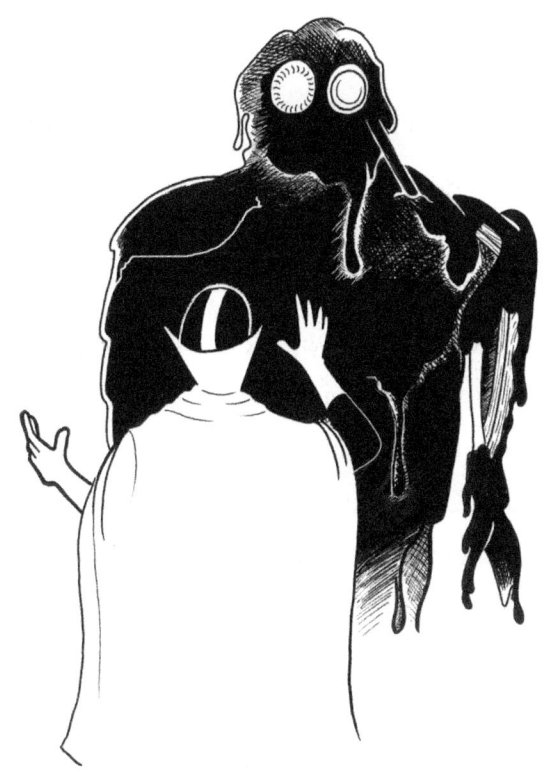

Chapter Twelve
THE BLACK & WHITE KNIGHT

It was beginning to get dark by the time he got his suit on and hopped in the back seat of the car. His dad drove him most of the way, then stopped the car before they reached the crowd and Norman slipped out. He flitted to a nearby shrub until the taillights of the car disappeared, then he popped out of the hedge and made his way toward the commotion.

Skunk-Guy headed to the scene of the uproar with a renewed spirit. Before he got very close to the crowd, a hand suddenly slapped down on his shoulder.

"It's about time you showed up."

He turned suddenly and found the same dark haired woman he had seen on TV.

"What took you so long?" she asked, pulling her hand away. She noticed that her hand was dripping wet.

"Sorry about that," Skunk-Guy said. "I didn't get a chance to dry my suit. It's clean though."

"Terrific," she muttered, wiping her hand on her leg. "My name is Rina Wells, and I owe you a big apology. You rescued me twice and I didn't treat you very nicely. I'm sorry."

"Oh!" Skunk-Guy stammered. "That's okay."

"I don't even remember your name," She confessed.

"I am the Stinking Stalker," he said boldly. "Well, that's my official name. But everyone else calls me Skunk-Guy."

"Well, Skunk-Guy," she said with a girlish curtsy, "you are my black and white knight in shining armor."

Skunk-Guy rubbed his hand behind his head awkwardly. His mask slid off to the side and he had to straighten it out.

She suppressed a giggle. "Now I think the police could use your help."

She led him through the crowd. The people stared at them as they walked past. But no one barred their way. In fact, the people actually stepped back, opening a path for them.

Skunk-Guy felt as though he *was* a knight being welcomed by the villagers who had hired him to slay the dragon.

They stopped in front of the yellow police tape that cordoned off the area. There was a uniformed policeman standing guard.

Rina spoke up, loud and clear. "Excuse us."

"What?" the officer asked.

"We need to talk to whoever is in charge here."

"The commissioner has his hands full right now," he told her.

"We can help him," Rina announced, looking over at her costumed partner.

"Look, this is not a good time for a publicity stunt," he stated sharply. "Now get lost."

Rina nudged Skunk-Guy to speak.

"Well... see..." he stammered. "I know about that thing... Uh... It's not really a thing. See, it's really some kind of a colony of little things. Hundreds, thousands, maybe even millions... of little things all linked together... into one big thing. It's actually pretty vulnerable to cold and it has a high sensitivity to smells."

Skunk-Guy took a deep breath. He was amazed at how much he sounded like Wendell just then. Rina was smiling with an *I told you so* glint.

The policeman stared at him for a long minute, then blurted out, "Just a minute," and ran off to get the Police Chief.

The Police Chief swaggered over to the yellow tape. He groaned when he saw Skunk-Guy standing there.

"What is this?" he growled.

"He said he can help us," the policeman told him.

"He can," Rina added.

The Chief sighed irritably. "Okay, what is that thing?" he barked.

"Well, I am not sure exactly what it is..."

The Chief rolled his head back in frustration.

"But I *do* know..." Skunk-Guy started to explain.

"Where did it come from?" the Chief interrupted abruptly.

"I-I... don't know," Skunk-Guy stammered.

"I don't have time for this," the Chief snapped and turned to walk away.

Skunk-Guy and Rina looked at each other helplessly.

Finally Rina shouted. "So, you've got this whole thing figured out then."

The Police Chief stopped and turned to answer. "We're working on it."

"You could at least give him a chance to explain himself," Rina insisted.

"Look, lady," the chief gave her a menacing glare, "that walking slime deposit sent two of my men to the hospital with severe chemical burns." He held up a smoldering police jacket. "I cannot afford to endanger citizens, no matter how... strangely they dress up."

Skunk-Guy involuntarily looked at his glove that had been stitched up from the burn he had experienced two days ago. He gulped nervously.

Just then a man stepped out from behind the Chief. He was wearing a beige safari suit with a name tag from the Children's Zoo.[*]

"Maybe we should hear him out," the man suggested.

The Chief relented. "All right, kid, what ya got?"

"Um," Skunk-Guy tried to sound convincing. "Ah, see, the thing knows me."

"Why doesn't that surprise me?" the Police Chief said.

"I found it when it was... well... smaller." Skunk-Guy's voice cracked. "It followed me home. See, I can make myself smell just like it smells. It trusts me."

---

[*] The Fort Wayne Children's Zoo is one of the top rated zoos in the country.

"I need to capture this… thing. Not teach it tricks," the Police Chief explained.

"Wait!" the zoo man thundered. "The Children's Zoo has a large underground shelter where the monkeys are put during the winter. It's large enough to hold that creature and it will be unoccupied till October. We could take it there."

"How would we get it there?" the chief asked.

"You could freeze it," Skunk-Guy suggested. "I used a fire extinguisher on it."

Rina grinned proudly. "Yeah, freeze it. Betcha didn't think of that."

"How would we pick it up?" the Chief said. "It must weigh a ton."

The zoo man asked Skunk-Guy, "Could you get it to follow you to the zoo?"

"Probably," Skunk-Guy told him.

"No, wait," the Chief said. "There's a rock salt company about half a mile down that road." He spoke to Skunk-Guy directly. "Could you get it to follow you inside one of their trucks?"

"Sure."

"All right, kid, let's go." The Chief nodded at the policeman, who lifted the tape directing Skunk-Guy to go under it.

Rina watched the Stinking Stalker and the police department head off into the woods.

"Make us proud, Skunk-Guy!" she shouted.

Ed parked the car and wandered into the crowd so he could keep an eye on his stinking son. When the policeman lifted the tape and

Skunk-Guy stepped through, Ed felt the pride of a father whose son is about to step up to the plate.

Janice and Barbara watched with great anxiety as the caped hero made his way into the woods and out of the camera's view.

"I could string your father up for talking me into this," Janice muttered.

"He'll be okay, Mom," Barbara assured her. "The police are right there, they won't let him get hurt."

Just then they saw on the TV screen a group of uniformed officers run out of the woods holding their noses.

～❦～

Skunk-Guy followed the Police Chief and the zoo man into the woods. They walked up to a group of officers.

"Where's the ah. . . thing?" the Chief asked.

One of the officers pointed down a dark path. "We've got it cornered down there."

The Chief turned to Skunk-Guy. "Okay son, do your stuff."

"Right!" Skunk-Guy shot back with a salute. Then he dashed down the dark path alone.

"What was that?" the policeman asked.

"Don't ask," the Chief grunted.

Skunk-Guy moved deeper into the woods until he stood face to face with the walking mound of muck.

"Yikes!" Skunk-Guy blurted out. "You're a lot taller in person."

The thing turned as though it were looking down at the Stinking Stalker.

"Hi," Skunk-Guy waved. "Remember me?"

The creature waved its arms and gurgled angrily, which sounded a lot like an enormous stomach growling.

"Settle down, settle down!" Skunk-Guy held his hands up to calm the thing. "We're old buddies, remember?"

"Oh, wait I forgot something." Skunk-Guy made himself smell just like the monster. The odor from the creature combined with that of stinking hero was so powerful that it drove the entire police force out of the woods.

But it was enough to calm the blobby brute. The creature lowered its arms and stood silent with its pop bottle eyes focused on Skunk-Guy.

"That's better," he told it.

Skunk-Guy looked around. "I think we're alone."

He stepped slowly around the monster, talking soothingly to put it at ease.

"Good monster, good ol' goo monster. We're just hanging out together. Just a couple of stinky buddies."

He stopped in front of it and asked, "Want to take a walk, huh?"

The thing tilted what would have been its head.

"Good, come on, follow me." Skunk-Guy moved slowly backward down the path he had come in on. He coaxed it with his hands. The huge slime creature followed timidly.

"We've done this before, remember?"

The hero and the monster walked out of the woods. A hush came over the crowd as everyone held their breath, as much in suspense as to avoid the smell.

"Don't pay any attention to them," Skunk-Guy told his companion. "Just follow me. Come on."

The two moved down the road slowly. The crowd followed them, up wind and at a safe distance. Many of the people were still holding their noses but the spectacle of the walking blob kept them all awestruck.

No one in the crowd was more amazed than Ed Flinch, who watched his son with great pride. It was all he could do to keep himself from nudging the man next to him and telling him that that was his son.

Janice and Barbara watched the TV coverage with wide-eyed amazement.

Rina Wells was standing next to the police chief with her fingers crossed behind her back.

Skunk-Guy led the muck monster all the way to the parking lot of the rock salt company. The waiting semi was idling noisily. The truck's back trailer was open, waiting for them to climb on board.

"Look at that," Skunk-Guy said as though he were talking to a small child. "We're going to go for a ride in that *biiig* truck."

The creature was skittish about getting near the semi. At that moment a beer bottle came flying through the air and hit the creature on the side of what should have been its head.

"Monster, Go Home!" a man shouted from the crowd.

The creature flailed its arms wildly. Skunk-Guy turned and moved cautiously toward the raging slime giant. His hands upheld in a passive gesture, he spoke softly to the...thing.

"Hold on, hold on, take it easy."

The monster swung his arms and knocked Skunk-Guy on to the pavement several feet away. Then it raised its arms high in the air and let out its gurgling growl.

Screams and pandemonium erupted from the crowd.

The creature focused on the black and white form lying on the pavement and charged angrily at Skunk-Guy. It took only two steps toward him when a blast of water from a high pressure fire hose blew the creature off balance. It staggered clumsily as the pressure of the water pushed it into one of the open loading dock doors. It disappeared inside the rock salt refinery.

A couple of paramedics and two firemen ran on to the scene. The paramedics went straight for the fallen hero, who was already sitting up on his own, while the firemen cautiously approached the loading dock where the thing had disappeared. A policeman was using a bull horn ordering the crowd to be quiet and stay back.

Skunk-Guy was helped to his feet by the paramedics.

"Hey kid, you all right?" one of them asked.

"Yeah," Skunk-Guy nodded. "I'll go get it."

"Wait!" the other one shouted. "You can't go in there."

"I have to," Skunk-Guy shouted back.

Skunk-Guy limped over to the bay door of the loading dock and was stopped by the firemen.

"We can't let you in there, son," the tallest of the two said, holding up his hand.

Skunk-Guy stopped, turned and looked at the wild mob. The commotion quieted down as the attention of the whole crowd fell on him. He realized that they were all depending on him. He knew that he was the one who was uniquely qualified to deal with this situation. All he needed to do was calm the creature and get it inside the waiting truck.

"The fate of the entire world," he told himself.

Janice was scolding the television set.

"Get out of there," she shouted to her son

"Mom, he can't hear you," Barbara told her.

"I'm warning you, young man," Janice continued, "if you go in there, you are so grounded."

Rina was silent. She felt responsible for getting Skunk-Guy into this situation. If anything happened to him, she would never be able to live with herself.

Ed was making his way through the crowd to rescue his son.

Suddenly the two firemen were on the ground gagging and choking, unable to breath through the rancid stench of decomposing meat mixed with ammonia that assaulted their noses.

Skunk-Guy turned back around and looked down at the wheezing firemen. "Sorry about that, guys, but I've got to do this."

Ed Flinch got to the front of the crowd just as Skunk-Guy disappeared into the refinery.

Chapter Thirteen
FACING THE BEAST

Skunk-Guy stepped carefully into the darkened building. The creature was nowhere to be seen. He stepped a little further in and looked around. There were six bay areas where trucks could back in. High above each bay was a huge holding tank where the rock salt would be collected and then poured through a long spout into the back end of the city salt trucks.

Along the back of the dock was a platform that was level to the floor of any open freight truck. The trucks could back in here and then be unloaded by a crew of dock workers.

Skunk-Guy spotted a set of stairs that led up to the loading platform. He tried to dash toward the stairs and slipped in the slime that was all over the cement floor. He was slipping and twisting spastically as he struggled to remain upright. He lunged toward the steps and grabbed hold of the metal hand rail, then grunted in relief.

"Just call me twinkle toes," he joked to himself.

He regained his balance and wiped the slime off of his shoes by scraping them on the edge of a step. He slowly ascended the stairs. Once at the top he felt a little taller and a smidgen safer. He scanned the area—no sign of his quarry.

There was only one bay door open and that was the one he and the creature had come through. That open door was the only source of light. He moved away from the light along the platform into the darker area of the bay.

"Come out, come out, wherever you are," he called as sweetly as he could.

"No one is going to hurt you," he added.

As he moved along, the shadows grew heavier, the dark closed in. He moved slower and slower. He was afraid to take a step for fear of falling off the loading platform.

Finally he resolved to bring the creature to him rather than going off in the dark. He remained motionless and concentrated on making himself smell like the creature.

He was grateful that he wasn't susceptible to his own odor.

After a painfully long wait, he heard something moving in the darkness below him: Wet, slappy, sloshy steps as the goo creature drew closer. It wasn't gurgling. That was a good sign.

"Hello there," he said as kindly as he could.

The dark in front of him grew denser. He knew the thing was standing right there.

"Did that big bad bottle scare you?" he asked blindly. "It's okay, I won't let them hurt you."

He practically popped his eyes trying to see it. He could just barely make out its silhouette. It looked like it was reaching out to him. Skunk-Guy couldn't tell if it was a friendly gesture, or if it intended to clobber him with its enormous wad of a hand.

"Easy, easy there." Skunk-Guy took two small steps forward.

Just then all the other huge bay doors roared open with a deafening rattle and clamor. Then light poured in around them, headlights and spotlights and even small-beamed flashlights. The creature jumped in terror and began waving its limbs defensively. Skunk-Guy was thrown backward by one of the creature's flailing arms.

He landed hard against a large green button on a control panel next to the platform. Suddenly a powerful stream of dry heavy rock salt came pouring down out of the overhead tank on top of the creature.

The pressure of the falling salt drove it to the floor. Then Skunk-Guy heard a strange sizzling and popping sound along with the roar of the pouring salt. The...thing was growing smaller and smaller in full view of the crowd that had surged forward to get a glimpse of the action.

Skunk-Guy tried to stop the salt by banging frantically on the control panel, flipping switches and pushing buttons, but nothing he did had any effect.

The salt kept pouring, and pouring, and pouring. Finally the last of it dropped through the rising salt dust and settled on the huge pile. Flowing out from under the salt was a lifeless blackish fluid. The muck monster was dead. It had dissolved like the wicked witch of the west.

Skunk-Guy stopped pounding on the panel and turned to look at the damage he had caused.

Four firemen charged in through the bay door, followed by a pair of police officers.

"Hurry!" Skunk-Guy called to them. "You gotta help it."

One fireman called back, "It's too late, kid. It's dead."

"You okay, son?" one of the policemen asked as he dashed up the steps.

"Yeah," Skunk-Guy answered sadly.

The policeman caught up to him. "You're quite the hero. You saved the city."

"I did?" He didn't feel like a hero. He felt like a killer.

"Come on," the officer said. "Let's get you out of here."

The two of them walked down the stairs and around the rock salt mound. Skunk-Guy couldn't help but feel sick about what was underneath all that salt.

As they stepped out onto the parking lot, the policeman announced to the crowd, "The creature is dead." Then he looked over at Skunk-Guy and added, "Thanks to the bravery of this young hero."

A cheer arose from the crowd and everyone applauded. Ed was clapping louder than anyone. He nudged the guy next to him and said, "That's my..." he caught himself, "hero."

Barbara and Janice were hugging each other and crying with joy.

Rina Wells ran out to her new-found hero and hugged him.

"You saved all of us this time," she said with admiration in her voice.

She took his hand and raised it in the air like the winner of a boxing match. Then she started chanting, "Skunk-Guy, Skunk-Guy, Skunk-Guy."

Almost at once the crowd joined her. Everyone was singing his name. The crowd swooped in on the two of them. A small group lifted Skunk-Guy to their shoulders and paraded him along the road.

Skunk-Guy felt a little better about what had happened, but he would always remember the terrible feeling he got when he finally slew the dragon and saw it die.

❧❧

Back at home Norman was embraced by the women of the family.

His mother hugged him so long and so hard he thought he was going to pop.

"If you ever pull a stunt like that again. . ." she finally said.

"Mom," he replied, "this is my destiny."

"Well, I have a thing or two to say about your destiny," she told him.

His sister hadn't hugged him since he rescued her a month ago. "That was pretty cool," she said. "But I'm glad you were wearing a mask. It will make school this fall a lot easier."

Ed put his hand on his son's shoulder. Norman stood wearing his Skunk-Guy suit minus the mask.

"You scared the living daylights out of us," Ed told him. Norman lowered his eyes, waiting for the scolding that was sure to come. "But I am very proud of how you handled yourself."

Norman looked up, surprised and pleased.

"You were a great help to a lot of people." He hugged his son.

Just then the phone rang. Barbara ran over and grabbed it.

"Hello," she said. "Oh yeah, sure." She held the phone out to Norman. "It's Wendell."

Norman grabbed it excitedly.

"Yeah," he said into the receiver.

"I saw what happened on TV," Wendell told him.

"Man, you should have been there," Norman told him. "The thing must have been ten feet tall, it was huge."

"It probably merged with the extra gunk that crawled out of the sewer this morning," Wendell explained.

"Do you think that there is any more of that stuff down there?" Norman asked

"I doubt it," Wendell stated. "The city water department will probably flush the sewers out real good, hopefully before something crawls out of someone's toilet."

"Eeoww!" Norman winced. "That's a scary thought."

"Well, if it did happen," Wendell said, "at least now we know how to stop it. It's just like pouring salt on a snail or a slug. The salt draws the water out of their bodies, and they shrivel up!"

"Yeah, it was pretty gross," Norman told him. "It made me feel kinda sick. One minute it was standing there and the next it was a pile of lifeless goo. All because I bumped into the wrong button. I was supposed to just lead it away. Instead I killed it."

"Well, it wasn't your fault exactly," Wendell said. "You're new at this. You'll get the hang of it."

"I hope so," Norman said sincerely

EPILOGUE

The next morning—after his chores—Norman rode his bike to Wendell's house. Mr. Higgins told him that Wendell was out in the greenhouse. When he got there he was astonished at what he found inside. The whole place had undergone a serious transformation.

Wendell peeped over the top of one of the tables from his place on the floor where he was untangling extension cords.

"Welcome to the new Secret Skunk Station of the Stinking Stalker," Wendell announced.

"Whoa," Norman blurted.

Wendell stood up as he explained, "Grandpa said that we could use this place for a secret clubhouse as long as we don't disturb his plants."

"This is perfect!" Norman said excitedly.

"Here, let me give you a tour of the place."

Wendell showed him the lab equipment he had set up on one table. The filing cabinet contained all their reference material, which consisted mostly of comic books. There was an old dresser.

"That's so you can keep an extra suit and some clothes stashed here," Wendell pointed out.

There was a small avocado-green freezer in the corner.

"That is for scientific specimens," Wendell explained, then added, "Here is our communication station."

There was a table cluttered with electronic stuff, including the now-working CB radio, a short wave radio and a police band radio, along with a collection of old walkie-talkies and a portable black and white TV.

"Oh, I gotta show you this." Wendell pulled out a bicycle frame that was tangled in a mass of loose wires and electronic gizmos. "I'm working on the *Skunk-Cycle*."

"This is so cool I hate to keep it a secret," Norman admitted.

"I figure it has to be a lot easier than digging up your yard."

"That idea didn't go over too well."

"Here's a key." Wendell handed it to his friend. "You can come in here any time. Just don't mess with Grandpa's plants over there."

Norman crossed his heart and saluted. "Skunk's honor."

"You're listening to WIFF radio. I am Rina Wells, the voice of late night Fort Wayne.

"As you probably all witnessed this past weekend, the Three Rivers Festival, and yes, our town itself, was saved from a hideous danger. We were saved by a brave young man in a strange costume.

"You've heard me speak on this show about searching for my guardian angel. Well, I found him. And he is here on the phone tonight. Will you give a warm welcome to my new found hero, and guardian of Allen County, Skunk-Guy the Stinking Stalker."

"Oh, geee!" Skunk-Guy's voice was filtered through the phone line and broadcast to all listeners.

"We are all in your debt, Skunk-Guy," Rina gushed.

"Well, I didn't exactly do it alone," Skunk-Guy pointed out. "In fact, if you hadn't insisted that I could help, the police would never have let me try."

"I saw how you handled the slime when it came out of the sewer," she said. "And I knew you were the man for the job."

"I did make friends with the goo a few days ago so I kinda knew how to handle it."

"You made friends with the goo?"

"Yeah…ah," Skunk-Guy stammered, trying to decide how much he could reveal without giving himself away. "It followed me home."

"You brought the goo creature to your house?"

"Not exactly to my house," he corrected. "It was my secret skunk station. But then it got away, and then it got bigger, and then I had to come in and take care of it."

"You did a great job, Skunk-Guy," she said proudly. "Now for anyone who missed you on TV this weekend, or your photo on the front page of the paper this morning, you have a cute black and white costume with a pull-over mask, cape and a skunk on your chest."

"That's right," he affirmed.

"So tell us about this special power you have."

"I can make myself smell like anything."

"He really can do this, folks. I've smelled him," she admitted. "So is this an inherited talent or something you developed on your own?"

"It was strictly by accident," he told her.

"Well, would you do us all a great favor, Skunk-Guy?"

"What?"

"Each night when you are on the prowl, would you call me here at the station and give us an update on your adventures?" she asked

"Really?"

"I would be proud to have you as a regular on my radio show," Rina said sincerely.

"I would be proud to *be* a regular on your radio show," he admitted.

"Fort Wayne needs to get to know the guy who is raising a stink about crime."

"Ouch!" Skunk-Guy groaned. "That was a bad pun."

"Are you saying my jokes stink?"

"About as bad as me," he answered.

At that moment, Rina realized that she didn't feel so alone any more. Norman meanwhile was thrilled that people were finally taking him seriously.

"I think this is the beginning of a beautiful friendship," she said, meaning it.

A SPECIAL NOTE
From the real Rina Wells

    I can't recall the exact day or time I first heard his voice. I don't remember what he said, or what I said in response. But I never will forget his unmistakable scent, that unforgettable aroma able to expand the constricted nasal boundaries dooming the rest of us to a merely mortal sense of smell and fun.

    For me, and for thousands of listeners tuning into the "After Midnight Club," my late night talk radio program broadcast on WOWO in Fort Wayne, Indiana in the late 1970s, Skunk-Guy wafted in like a breath of -- if not fresh, then definitely stimulating -- air.

Skunk-Guy's frequent reports on his crime-fighting exploits in that hotbed of perdition, Allen County, became a highlight of the show. Listeners enjoyed the tales of the Stinking Stalker, and many applied to become members of his Skunk Squad, an elite corps dedicated to eradicating evil.

Many doubted his existence, assuming Skunk-Guy was just some nut with a telephone and insomnia. I always believed there was a real guy behind the voice, a guy who felt (and smelt) strongly about setting things right in the world, a fella who wanted to bring justice to the maligned and the maligners to justice.

My faith was rewarded but once, when I met Skunk-Guy in person. He stood before me in the WOWO lobby, resplendent in his black-and-white Skunk Suit. For a moment the air was filled with a musky scent; I felt lightheaded, and nearly swooned. He took my hand, and then, with a flick of his cape, disappeared into the elevator.

I never saw his face. But I knew then that wherever evil reigned, wherever there was a wrong to be righted, there Skunk-Guy would be, sniffing out trouble and saving the day for the olfactorily-challenged of the world. He is a superhero in every scent of the word.

Maureen Mecozzi
Skunkscout #46-711-90

ABOUT THE AUTHOR

Michael holds an Associates Arts degree from the American Academy of Dramatic Arts. He is an actor, writer and illustrator, as well as a closet comic book geek. At the tender age of fourteen he created his own alter ego, known as Skunk-Guy. Stitching together a costume, he conducted night time patrols on the streets of his home town, Fort Wayne, Indiana, where he was dubbed "The Black Knight" by the FWPD. Now many years later, he has retired from active super-hero duty and lives peaceably in Fort Wayne with his wife, Cindy, and their daughter, Josette. *The Sensational Slime Saga* is his second novel.

www.ingramcontent.com/pod-product-compliance
Lightning Source LLC
Chambersburg PA
CBHW031401040426
42444CB00005B/370